# Contents

# Part Two – *New Media, New Behaviours*

# Introduction

Developments in computer networking over the last decade have provided language with a whole range of new spaces in which to work and play. The studies in this collection investigate the ways in which language use and language itself is adapting to the new computer-based media through which it is increasingly channelled. Some of the papers were adapted from presentations at a workshop on Computer Mediated Communication organised by Lyn Pemberton at the Sociolinguistics Symposium 1997 in Cardiff, others are developed from presentations at the Writing and Computers Conference run by both the editors in Brighton 1997 and others were commissioned specifically for the collection. The aim has been to give coverage of as wide a range of approaches and phenomena possible at every level of interest to students of language, from the mechanics of replicating paralinguistic features in email to the pragmatics of multilingual communication and from the grammatical features of Web page anchor text to the negotiation of meaning in an email discussion on traditional song. The approaches used in the studies range from corpus-based statistics through to experimental psycholinguistics, social identity theory, systemic linguistics and conversation analysis. One informal measure of the diversity of approaches is the amount of overlap in bibliographical references: only one work, Sherry Turkle's *Life on Screen*, was referenced in more than one chapter, vividly demonstrating the range of quite different perspectives which can usefully be employed in studying the domain.

The papers in the first part of the collection focus on issues of language structure in networked and computer-supported communication. The first two chapters, though very different in emphasis, share a concern with the written representation of complex conceptual structures. In Chapter 1, Jaime Henriquez describes the subtle interplay between the implementation choices made by the developers of the World Wide Web, particularly the hypertext link mechanism, and the way readers engage with web documents. Taking a writer's perspective, he uses the notion of web authoring as 'writing without prepositions' to suggest ways for both writers and software designers to overcome the new problems which people face when reading web documents.

One of the most promising uses for the WWW is, of course, learning. In Chapter 2, Bernard Scott introduces Conversation Theory as a way of modelling complex knowledge domains and suggests that it is particularly relevant for course design and communication in a hypertext environment such as the web. Conversation Theory offers a principled approach to addressing some of the concerns expressed by Henriquez over the undefined semantics of the current generation of hypertext links in web documents.

In Chapter 3, Einat Amitay investigates the language used in the anchors of hypertext links in web documents, describing, for instance, the different effects of using a definite rather than an indefinite article when referring to a linked page. The incorporation of what are essentially operating instructions into a written document is quite a novel phenomenon (paper pages don't usually include a 'turn here' instruction, after all, although 'See Figure 1' comes close) and as in several other chapters, a new set of conventions is captured here as they evolve.

Genre is a central structuring notion for linguists and will surely be a rich area for investigation as computer-mediated discourses develop and establish their conventions. In Chapter 4, Helmut Gruber presents a close analysis of a particular type of behaviour, citation, in two discussion lists that by many criteria would be judged to belong to the same genre. Citation behaviour differs to a marked degree between these lists, however, suggesting that sub-genres are already beginning to appear.

Pirkko Raudaskoski's study of Internet Video Conferencing in Chapter 5 broadens the range of media under consideration to include speech and video. The focus here is on text, usually considered the 'poor relation' in the technologically oriented world of video conferencing, demonstrating how the features of on-screen text, particularly its persistence, can be used to advantage by participants, in conjunction with newer media.

If there is one thing we now know for sure about computer-mediated communication it is that CMC texts share characteristics of both written and spoken language and that users of email in particular use devices such as 'smilies' to give a spoken flavour to their texts. In Chapter 6, Robert Fouser, Narahiko Inoue and Chungmin Lee deliver a corrective to the widespread anglocentricity of Internet studies with an account of the differences between the uses of such 'orality mechanisms' across three languages and cultures - English, Japanese and Korean. They discuss the interplay between the take-up and development of orality in CMC and the writing systems, word-processing technology and ultimately the rhetorical traditions of the cultures in question.

The second half of the collection is concerned with the language-based behaviour of users of a range of CMC technologies. In Chapter 7, Zazie Todd and Stephanie Walker present a study of a multilingual chat facility, concentrating in particular on its potential for language learning and exploring the attitudes, both positive and negative, displayed towards other languages amongst users. Sandra Harrison's study in Chapter 8 is a mapping of Brown and Levinson's work on politeness into the domain of email. A close analysis of messages from a discussion group reveals the use of a wide range of positive politeness techniques to promote a 'safe' environment for discussion and to create group cohesion. In Chapter 9, Heather Matthews studies the interplay between transactional and interactional aspects of the use of discussion groups and finds that even those users who claim to be pursuing work-related goals in fact engage in much behaviour that is socially-oriented. Matthews' focus on the importance of the playful behaviour afforded by networks is a useful counter-balance to the work-oriented studies of CMC carried out under the umbrella of Computer Supported Co-operative Work (CSCW).

In Chapter 10, Sonja Launspach uses a set of exchanges from a group concerned with traditional singing to study the rôle of context in the negotiation of a disputed term. She argues that the lack of overlap in contexts between contributors to the thread, in which individuals brought their own strong and diverse assumptions to the interpretation of the disputed term, was a major factor in a breakdown of communication in the group. This type of negotiation of meaning can be particularly fraught when metaphorical language is used and users need to be aware of potential difficulties if communication is to succeed.

Jacqui Taylor's study in Chapter 11 focuses on the effects of group identity and self identification on behaviour within email groups. It was found that contrary to previous findings, users who could be personally identified in fact tended to produce more uninhibited contributions than those who remained anonymous. Taylor argues for more research to allow for a 'culmination of results' and a clarification of inconsistent results across studies. The rate of change in CMC behaviour is such that a rolling programme of this type of research effort is surely needed if we are to understand the effects of the new media on language and behaviour.

The final chapter is a reminder that whereas most CMC studies are concerned with communication *through* a computer, other important category of CMC might be termed communication *for* a computer. Luís Pérez-González describes the effects on natural interaction that arise when one participant, in this case a call taker for an ambulance service, is constrained by the demands of software which processes the caller's information. Linguistic analysis here is of immediate practical use, as a description of the structure and content of the caller's contributions can be a useful tool in weeding out bogus calls. However, Pérez-González also shows that the constraints imposed by the software can result in a mismatch of interactional styles, with the call taker's need for efficiency at odds with the needs of an emotional and confused caller. This is obviously a point that must be taken into account in the design of human-computer dialogues.

Both the first and last chapters of the collection point to lessons for the design of systems, and this may be a useful topic on which to conclude this introduction. The software we use for communication, whether in Chat rooms, video conferences, email or the web, is of very recent manufacture and is far from fixed in design. CMC researchers are engaged in the exciting work of observing as practices change and conventions form, but they are also in a strong position, if they will take up the challenge, to influence through their observations the design of the very software via which we will communicate in the future.

*Lyn Pemberton*
*Simon Shurville*
University of Brighton

# – Part One –
# *New Media, New Structures*

## 1. One-way Doors, Teleportation and Writing without Prepositions: an analysis of WWW hypertext links

Jaime Henriquez

As a method of communication, the World Wide Web is unusual in several ways - in its delivery (by computer rather than printed page, radio waves, etc.), speed, audience, multimedia aspects, interactivity, connections to databases, and so on. Attempting to assess the effects of this chimera on communication is daunting in part because it is difficult to know what new aspect to examine first. As a starting point, I have chosen to examine the web's hypertext link, in its current form.

New media create new forms of communication. Each medium both enhances and restricts different aspects of communication. The key to understanding how communication via the web differs from other forms of communication lies in the *link*. If we look closely at the link, we find in its traits clues to the ways in which communication changes when conducted over this new medium.

### 1.1. The role of links

To begin with, a World Wide Web link is a connection between some point on one web page (which I'll call the A page) and a point (usually the beginning) of any other web page (the B page). When reading the A page, with an appropriate web browser program, clicking on the link causes the B page to be displayed instead.

Links exercise a considerable influence on what material a reader sees, and in what order. While there is no limit to the length of a web page, most are no longer than a few printed pages. When the reader finishes a page, links provided by the author offer the most obvious options for continuation, though not the only ones. Any page which can be reached by link can be reached directly, without the link, so long as its address (its Universal Resource Locator, or URL) is known. Directly specifying the URL of the page you want to see requires some knowledge, however, and those who regard computers as inherently mysterious frequently choose not to take this route, especially as URLs are typically a 20-30 character near-nonsense string which must be typed in precisely as given. Clicking on a link is easier.

Web page URLs are inherently uninformative - they indicate nothing about what you will see when the page is displayed (1). Telephone numbers pose a similar problem, giving little or no indication of who will answer the phone if you dial the number, or how you might find that person by some other means (by mail, for example). The lack is corrected by telephone directories, or address books, which supply some or all of that missing information. Links do for web pages what directories or address books do for telephones, i.e. they give some information about what is on the B page. The link implies, at a minimum, that the author of the A page thought the B page to be of some interest, for some reason. One can call any phone number at random, but the majority of calls are *to* someone, made with the help of a directory of some sort. Similarly, most web pages are displayed with the help of a link. Links invite the reader to new pages and, as we shall see in the discussion of the link's directionality, the invitation is a forceful one.

Links, then, have a strong impact on a reader's choices and, ultimately, what s/he sees. An analysis of the World Wide Web link can shed light on the similarities and differences of communicating via the web rather than other media, and at the same time suggest guidelines for creating effective web pages. While some of these conclusions and suggestions will be familiar to developers of web content, even those who are familiar with the suggestions may profit by a better understanding of the reasons behind them.

Three aspects of the World Wide Web link have strong effects on writing. These characteristics can create problems for both authors and readers. They are:
- the link is directional;
- the link is instant;
- the link is generic.

## 1.2. The Directional Link

A link in a chain looks and acts the same regardless of which way one travels the chain to get to it. From either direction, it is just as strong or weak. A web link, on the other hand, is different when seen from the A page or the B page. On the A page, a link is indicated by highlighting of text and/or by a change in the cursor. On the B page, there is nothing. Going from A to B is following the path of less resistance, going 'downstream,' if you will. Going from B to A, perhaps via a Back button, is travelling 'upstream' — not impossible certainly, but a very different proposition.

The directional nature of links is crucial to the rapid growth of the web. It means that anyone, regardless of who or where they are, can create an enduring link to a page which interests them, without the permission or even the knowledge of the page's author. For an author, making information available in this way comes with a one-time cost. Since there is no complementary link back *to* the A page, links to the author's page require no work on their part. The only effort is on the part of the person who wishes to link to it. This directionality was an inspired decision by the creators of the

World Wide Web, one which enhances the flow of information via computers. It does, however, have a down side.

## Loss of Context

The author of a web page need not know who is setting up a link to their page; it is also true that the author *cannot* know this. Consequently, the reader's entry path is unpredictable. There is no way to know what web page a reader just came from, or what is likely to be in their mind because of it. Writers of books have some assurance that attentive readers are following the sequence laid out for them in previous pages. Even if readers are less than cooperative, authors can comfort themselves with the knowledge that they have provided a sequence of which readers can avail themselves if they wish. Writers of web pages may also have provided such a sequence, but they have considerably less assurance that readers followed it or are even aware of it.

To be sure, book readers may be interrupted or may lose the thread of the author's argument. But with printed material the remedy is apparent. The thread exists and its location is known - it is on the previous pages. Web page readers come to a page from an unknown and unknowable previous page. As a result, web page authors cannot count on readers having seen, or being able to easily retrieve, preparatory material. Context built up over several pages — essential for allowing an author to make complex arguments or clarify subtle concepts — suddenly becomes unreliable. Directional links reduce an author's 'reach' to a single web page, turning writers of books or articles into writers of one-page flyers. Arguably, only subjects and subject treatments capable of being covered on a single web page are truly suited to the medium as it exists.

Providing preparatory material for readers to absorb and refer back to if necessary seems hardly worth the author's time, because some percentage of readers will not enter by way of the author's A page, but rather from someone else's A page, or from a page of search results. 'As stated in the last chapter' and similar helpful asides lose their effectiveness. The overall effect on readers is to deprive them of context. The effect on authors is to limit their options for helping readers master difficult concepts. Furthermore, since readers may arrive unprepared, authors must either write for a general audience which lacks any specialised knowledge, or risk irritating those who cannot handle (and did not expect) more advanced material.

Two current aspects of the web aggravate the problem of directional links:
* full-text searching;
* the way browser programs such as Navigator or Explorer display pages.

## Full-text searching

A full-text search produces a page of links to pages whose text contains one or more words specified by the reader. Frequently a search yields thousands of links, the majority of which are irrelevant. The ones which *are* relevant are just as likely to dump the reader into the middle of a sequence as at the beginning. Search results from a subject-indexed search engine (such as Yahoo) are much more likely to lead a reader to introductory material (often home pages), and give authors some opportunity to provide context. However, full-text search engines (Lycos, AltaVista, etc.) are less labour-intensive, more current and more common.

## The palimpsest display

The developers of the first web browsers decided, probably correctly, that web page creators would want as much screen space as possible to display their information. To accommodate this desire, pages linked from (A pages) are completely replaced by pages linked to (B pages). The computer screen is used as a palimpsest - each page is erased by its successor. This delivery method has its drawbacks, however, which tend to enhance the problematic nature of directional links. Preparatory pages which the reader happens upon vanish as soon as they move on to another page. Any important information must be retained in memory. So too must the URL of the vanished page, if the reader has any desire or need to return to it. Browser programs assist the reader by providing a log of links to pages travelled, but this "backing up" process, typically via the Back button, is not entirely dependable, as pages disappear from memory unpredictably.

Both directional links and delivery via palimpsest threaten context, the former by making the previous page unknown, the latter by erasing the potentially helpful previous page. Any sense of history is at risk, with the only record of where you came from in your memory or your computer's memory. Neither one is as dependable as a sequence of pages bound together.

Loss of context is disorienting. When one is in search of information in an unfamiliar field, the web can feel like a carnival fun-house - you begin in a room with several closed doors (or links); you pick a door, enter the next room (or page), and the door you by which you came in promptly disappears, replaced by one or more new closed doors. Any sense of direction is quickly lost, as your perspective is limited to your immediate surroundings. Soon your only option is to just pick a door in the hope that the exit will find you. Similarly, searching the web can be disheartening - clicking on promising links in the  forlorn hope that things will become clearer, until you either lose interest in the question or forget what you were looking for.

## Suggestions to alleviate the effects

The directional nature of links is inherent in the web, but that fact should not prevent us from trying to lessen its deleterious effects. Full-text search engines and palimpsest delivery, on the other hand, are implementation decisions, which can and should be re-examined when they prove to be problematic. Equally capable of change are browser implementations of existing HTML tags.

The sequence, or 'previous page' problem can be handled through an implementation of the 'LINK REL=next' or 'REL=prev' tag. Currently these are little used, as most browsers ignore them. Assigning keys to link automatically to the logically next and previous pages (the right and left arrow keys are good possibilities) would encourage authors to use these tags, and permit readers who land in the middle of a sequence to follow it forward or backward with ease.

A second approach to the unknowable 'previous page' would be to modify browser programs so that any link to a subsidiary page in a website defaults to the site's main home page, or to the page specified with the 'LINK REL=start' tag. There would have to be an easy way to override this default (option key, right mouse button, etc.) and force the specific subsidiary page to come up, but by defaulting to an 'entry' page, links would normally lead to introductory and preparatory material, providing some orientation for readers. Such a modification would automatically affect search result pages, as well. In a sense, for those not seeking a specific page, such a change would make 'books' out of the single pages of the web.

An approach to the problem of palimpsest delivery would be to offer an easy way, now implemented in some browser programs, to open a linked page in a new window, and offset the window several pixels on the screen (down would allow the title to remain visible), thereby making it easier to recall pages the reader may wish to refer back to. The inclusion of frames (multiple pages displayed at once) in the HTML 4.0 recommendation opens up the possibility of using frames for this purpose as well and this is becoming a popular approach.

## 1.3. The Instant Link

Perhaps the greatest wonder of the Internet's data transfer method is that data from across the world is just as accessible as data from next door, and likely to arrive just as quickly. Since web links cause data transfer, as a web page is copied from its server to the user's computer, the same novelty applies. While the link is not exactly instant, it is largely insensitive to the distance between server and client (the user's browser). The time you have to wait for a page to be displayed varies, but distance plays a relatively minor role in this variation. While this dramatically increases a person's access to information (and access to audience), it also has an interesting side-effect - where once distance carried meaning, it can no longer do so.

### *Loss of a meaningful continuum*

The reader clicking an a web link may think in terms of 'going' to the new page. But this is not like going to the store or into town. There is no sense of distance travelled. It is more like teleportation or instantaneous relocation. One minute you're here; for an indeterminate (though usually short) period you're nowhere; then you're there.

Over the years we have become accustomed to distance and it is frequently used to carry meaning. In a book, certain material is in 'Chapter 1' by design - it is the closest to the front cover and is correspondingly important. The relegation of information to the back of the book also carries meaning for readers. The first (closest) material is treated differently than the more distant; both authors and readers know this. General interest information tends to be first, followed by more specialised material. All this meaning vanishes as readers teleport from web page to web page - each new page seems equally important (or unimportant).

On the web there is no inherent spatial arrangement of pages upon which we, as authors or readers, can rely. All points are equidistant, equally available. Relationships between pages are arbitrary, not spatial. These relationships, then, must be created by authors, and must then be communicated to readers. What is lost to teleportation must be either replaced or done without.

## No boundaries

Space involves more than simply near and far; spatial organisation also involves boundaries, i.e. the division of space into areas. As well as distance, teleportation removes boundaries and this has implications for the organisation of information and its retrieval.

Material within a boundary is related. It often has a single author or a single subject. Furthermore, it has an structure distinct from the material outside the boundary. The boundary both encloses and informs - 'herein lies something different, something new'. In addition, the boundary often provides information about its contents. The common injunction notwithstanding, books *are* judged by their covers. A carefully designed cover draws in the intended audience, and discourages those who are likely to be disappointed by the contents. It communicates the subject, the author, the treatment, and the expected level of knowledge.

Instant links eliminate boundaries and thus eliminate another form of preparatory information. Without a 'cover,' authors lose a prime opportunity to warn readers of prerequisites, quantity and complexity of material, area covered (or not), language, and intended audience. Either authors must provide this information in some other way, or readers must go without.

## No boundary negotiation

A lack of boundaries also affects the actions of readers. Where there are no boundaries, there is no need to negotiate boundaries. Putting down one book and beginning to read another is very different from clicking a link. Not only is more preparatory information involved in the former, more preparatory actions are involved. The ease with which one can 'teleport' around the web makes the process of moving from page to page less noticeable and since all pages are equally available, the process of moving from area to area, crossing 'boundaries', is equally unmarked. This lowered effort has a dramatic effect upon who reads a web page, and how.

When a process can be accomplished with less effort, it can be more casually engaged in. A casual reader is an uncommitted reader. This implies not only that readers of web pages will quickly click away from a page that does not meet their (immediate) need; it also implies that they will casually click *to* a page that may not be relevant since, even if the page is found to be irrelevant, the cost is quite small.

Directional links, as noted above, make it difficult to provide preparatory information: instant links make it seem less worthwhile to provide any. If readers appear to lose less by ignoring preparatory information, they are more likely to do so. That this lowered cost is deceptive (the immediate effort is less, but the effort over the long run will likely be more) is easy to overlook. Consequently, readers are less likely to *select* a web page, and more likely simply to *encounter* it.

Two fundamental issues in communication are affected by this aspect of the web - what is the point being made, and who is the audience. As to the former, the instant link encourages readers to freely and unremarkedly mix authors. An author's points become entangled with those of other authors. As to the latter, authors cannot focus as tightly on an audience. Given the global span of the web, you may well get more readers, but they will be less self-selectedly your audience, less likely to already know something about the subject.

### Suggestions to alleviate the effects

The inability to use distance to carry meaning does not alter the usefulness of spatial metaphors in organising web pages. It does mean, however, that such metaphors are arbitrary, not reinforced by physical distance. As a result, organisation on the web must be carefully communicated to the reader and reinforced, preferably on every page, if it is to be effective. Obliteration of boundaries can be addressed through the home-page default discussed previously. By preferentially presenting readers with a 'cover' page, much of the lost information can be replaced. The effects of instant links on the audience of a web page can be treated by, again, writing for a general audience where possible, and by providing author, subject, and treatment information on each page. A carefully chosen title and author line, repeated on each page, could well serve this purpose.

## 1.4. The generic link

The transition from one WWW page to another, if all goes well, is complete, immediate and colourless. No particular relationship is specified between the pages - it is simply a juxtaposition. Nothing is implied but a replacement of the old by the new. As a consequence, using a link to connect two pages on the web is like trying to write without prepositions or any connecting word or phrase. The well-thumbed thesaurus is set aside in favour of a generic connection, like the 'And now this . . .' of television announcers.

Web links are designed to be generic. Quoting from a preliminary specification for HTML 4.0, '. . . links have no inherent semantics; they just associate a source and a destination.' Links can be given some semantic specificity with the REL and REV attributes of the <LINK> and <A> tags, which allow authors to sequence pages or specify a glossary, for example, but these options are as yet little used by browsers (and hence unavailable to readers) (2). The upshot is that generic links leave authors with a seriously impoverished lexicon for connecting the contents of web pages.

Simple juxtaposition of pages like images in a film montage is a far cry from carefully crafted connections specifying, for example, 'A, therefore B' or 'B is evidence for A' or 'despite A, B' or 'usually A, but sometimes B.' Lacking some additional specificity, readers are left with 'A, then B,' which can be interpreted in a multitude of ways.

### The value of being specific

The value of specifying relationships is well-known to teachers of writing. Specificity makes it possible to communicate, to foster understanding in another person's mind. In the process, it forces an often fruitful reconceptualisation of ideas which are rarely as clearly conceived as they seemed. Unfortunately for teachers, the generic nature of Web links offers an easy out for the writer - 'let the reader make the (obvious) connection.' That this is both lazy and dangerous must be emphasised.

Ultimately, writing either web pages or printed pages is a communicative act, intended to transmit *something* from author to reader. While the success or failure of the act can perhaps only be judged at the reader's end, I believe it is the duty of the author to try their best to ensure that the reader comprehends the author's understanding of the subject. Anything less short-changes the reader. Taking away the author's thesaurus makes the task considerably more difficult, although, in this case, and to a degree, it may be appropriate.

### Limits to specificity on the web

On the web, there is a limit to the specificity possible. Web documents are computer-based, retained in magnetic or electric memory. As such they are more easily changed than printed documents. In a sense, they are less stable. Ease of updating can lead to frequent changes, jeopardising Tuesday's precise relationship by the week's end. Aggravating the problem is the issue of control of material on the web. With careful choice of content and organisation, it is possible to specify relationships between pages under your control, but if updates are done by someone else, or if links go to pages controlled by someone else, all bets are off. The problem of lack of specificity in web links is real, but any solution must recognise that the appropriate level of specificity may be different for the web than for print.

### Counteracting the effect of the generic link

The generic link's effect is simple - vague connection. Communication aimed at understanding requires a high degree of specificity. If a link is to be anything more than a juxtaposition, the information which would otherwise be provided by well-chosen connecting phrases must be provided in some other way. At the same time, the ephemeral nature of the web limits the degree to which authors can be specific.

Given the directional nature of links, it is not possible to specify the relationship of two pages from the B page, since the reader's A page is unknown. Consequently, an author's only option is to provide specific information about a link on the A page, information which indicates the nature of the relationship between the A and B pages, and identifies the source of the B page (if different from the A page). Such information may be unnecessary for a knowledgeable audience but, as noted above, there is a strong likelihood that unprepared readers will see the page as well. No reader of any web page should have to ask 'Why am I *here*?' To give an example, some readers would not immediately understand the relation of an Immunology graduate program to the 'CDC.' Providing the full name, Centers for Disease Control, gives some indication of the relationship between the two pages. Placing the link in a list labelled 'National Health Organizations' provides even more. Additionally, some recent versions of browsers can display the TITLE attribute of the link, giving another method for providing information. Any or all of these methods can be used to make up for the problem of 'writing without prepositions.'

The unstable nature of web pages can be addressed by a careful choice of B pages. Links to the home or entry page of a site are more likely to remain usable over time; in addition, they often provide preparatory information useful to your reader. On the other hand, there is considerable convenience in linking directly to the relevant subpage. B pages should be chosen with a careful balance between this convenience and the risk of broken links and baffled readers.

## 1.5. Conclusion

Links provide interactivity for the reader, allow choice and involvement, and permit multiple paths to information, thereby supporting multiple reader points-of-view, and encouraging access to new information. As the preceding analysis has shown, web links also place a greater load on the reader. Readers have to carry or supply more context, comprehend and remember arbitrary structures, deal with a lack of preparatory information, and cope with unspecified relationships between pages.

It is important that we, as web developers and web page authors, do whatever we can do to ease the reader's burden in this new medium, either directly, through improved page and site design, or indirectly, through urging the makers of web browsers to make appropriate changes. Realising that web links are like one-way doors, that travel by link is like teleportation, and that writing with links is like writing without prepositions can help us remain mindful of the problems as well as the potential of the World Wide Web.

### Notes

1. By convention, URLs may provide some information to those familiar with how to read them, but there is no guarantee of its utility.
2. It is also the case that authors and readers tend to *assign* meanings to inherently generic links, creating, by their shared understanding of the task, classes of links, which are widely, if only vaguely, understood.

# 2. Knowledge content and narrative structure

## Bernard Scott

## 2.1 Introduction

Many of the ideas expressed in this paper are inspired by and derived from Conversation Theory (CT) as developed in a number of publications by the late Gordon Pask  (Pask, Scott and Kallikourdis, 1973; Pask, 1975, 1976; Scott, 1993).  In an early outline of the scope of CT, Pask (1972) demarcated a sub-theory of conversational domains.  This sub-theory is predicated on the assumption that conversations are about something; the conversation has a subject matter, a topic to be addressed.  The sub-theory of conversational domains has itself many ramifications and research questions, including:

• how do conversational domains come into being and evolve?
• what constitutes a conversational domain as a coherent knowable, whole?
• how may the structure of a conversational domain be analysed and described?

It is argued in this paper that, whilst narrative structures, stories and expositions can be described in a variety of ways using scripts, frames and general schemas, by carrying out 'after the event' analyses of discourse and written text, those structures represent only a limited view of the knowledge content of a conversational domain (see, for examples of these approaches, Flood, 1984, and Britton and Graesser, 1996). What is needed, and what is provided in Pask's sub-theory of conversational domains, is a canonical way of modelling the structure of knowledge content such that all possible narrative structures may be revealed and articulated as particular forms.

In order to keep the scope of the paper within tractable bounds, the focus is on the composition of expository narratives. This avoids the need to discuss and classify different narrative genres. There is reference to different forms within the class of expository narratives. If spaced permitted, it would have been particularly interesting to relate these to the classification of sub-genres of expository narrative, proposed by Davies and Greene (1984). Typical examples  of expository narrative include a student writing an essay, a teacher designing a course or preparing a particular lesson, and the exchanges that take place in tutorial conversations where teacher and learner explain their understanding of topics one to another.

In the first part of the paper, there is a brief introduction to the main concepts of CT. This is followed by the construction of a generic model for the knowledge content of conversational domains. Novel aspects of the model are that, in a unified framework, it distinguishes conceptual and procedural knowledge, relations of entailment and analogy and hierarchical and heterarchical conceptual structures.

The second part of the paper considers how, by adopting a particular perspective on a body of knowledge, a class of expository narratives may be distinguished that are semantically equivalent but structurally varied in well-defined ways.

Finally, it is noted that the model may be interpreted dynamically, as a model of conceptualisation and directed thought, incorporating individual differences. In their studies of students' learning, Pask and Scott (1972), using a 'teachback' assessment procedure, showed that not only do individuals adopt characteristic strategies when coming to know a body of subject matter but that there are also characteristic differences in the ways in which expository narratives are composed.

## 2.2 Conversation Theory

Although CT may be elaborated as a general theory of human communication and social interaction, here, for the sake of brevity, we shall interpret it as a theory of learning and teaching, in which one participant (the teacher) wishes to expound a body of knowledge to a second participant (the learner). We shall refer to parts of the body of knowledge as 'topics', reserving the term 'concept' for the mental procedures that indicate understanding of a topic. We shall refer to particular instantiations or models of topics as 'relations', defined with respect to a canonical universe of discourse or modelling facility.

Pask's formal definition of a concept is that it 'is a procedure for recognising, reproducing or maintaining a relation' (see Figure 1).

Corresponding to the idea of a body of subject matter being a knowable, coherent whole, Pask distinguishes cognitive organisations that are self-reproducing system of concepts (see Figure 2). Pask refers to such systems as *psychological (p-) individuals*.

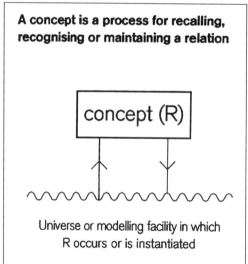

Figure 1. Pask's formal definition of a concept.

A major innovation of conversation theory is that psychological unities are not necessarily in one-to-one correspondence with biological unities. Pask refers to the latter as *mechanical (m-) individuals*. Thus one brain may house several conceptual systems as p-individuals and several brains may house one conceptual system as a single p-individual (as in the 'distributed cognition' of a team at work).

Figure 3 shows what Pask calls the 'skeleton' of a conversation. It depicts the situation in which two participants, learner and teacher, are in conversation about a topic. By distinguishing particular concepts from the systems of which they are a part, it is possible to distinguish *how* and *why* levels of explanation and understanding, as follows.

The horizontal connections represent verbal, symbolic exchanges. Pask argues that all such exchanges have, as a minimum, two logical levels. In the figure these are shown as the two levels *how* and *why*. The *how* level is concerned with how to do a topic, how to recognise it, construct it, maintain it and so on. The *why* level is concerned with explaining or justifying what a topic means in terms of other topics.

Participants may also interact non-verbally through a shared world or modelling facility. This is a place where topics can be instantiated or modelled. Here the teacher can demonstrate the *how* of a topic as a set of procedures and in turn the learner can show evidence of understanding a topic by solving problems and constructing models.

Pask refers to learning about *why* as *comprehension learning* and learning about *how* as *operation learning*. Laurillard (1993) provides a more elaborated account of each of the twelve possible exchanges that make up the skeleton of a conversation, interpreted for the kinds of learning conversation that take place in Higher Education. Here, a brief example will have to suffice.

Consider topics in chemistry. A teacher may provide explanations of why certain processes take place and may request that a learner teaches back his or her conceptions of why certain things happen. A teacher may give verbal accounts of how to bring about certain events or ask a learner to provide such an account. A teacher may model or demonstrate certain processes or events. A learner may be asked to carry out experiments or other practical procedures pertaining to particular events or processes.

In Pask's terminology, if a learner can successfully explain the *why* and demonstrate

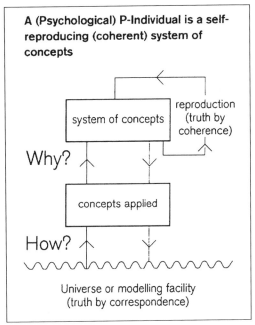

Figure 2. A conceptual system (p-individual).

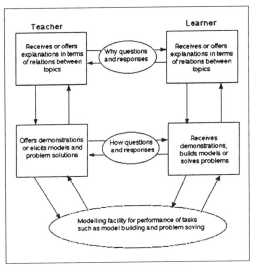

Figure 3. The 'skeleton' of a conversation.

the *how* of a topic, then he or she is said to *understand* that topic. Armed with these constructs and distinctions we are now in a position to construct a model for the structure of knowledge.

## 2.3   A model for the structure of knowledge

Essentially, what we are summarising here is an 'algebra of understanding' (Pask, Kallikourdis and Scott, 1973).

 We begin with the basic idea that a body of knowledge or subject matter consists of a set of topics related one to another.  We distinguish two basic forms of relations between topics - entailment relations and relations of analogy.  Examples of entailment relations are shown in Figure 4, while the analogy relation is shown in Figure 5. Graphical representations of relations of entailment and analogy are referred to as entailment structures.

 Figure 4 is a simple entailment structure, one without analogies. It shows that understanding topic A entails the prior understanding of topics B and C.

 Figure 5 shows that topics in one universe of discourse are related analogically to topics in a second universe of discourse. The important point to appreciate is that the existence of analogy relations reveals a variety of learning routes (or, as later, possible narrative forms).

 In the example, there are three main choices - learning about universes 1 and 2 separately and then learning about the form of the analogy that relates them or learning about one of the universes, say universe 1, then learning about the form of the

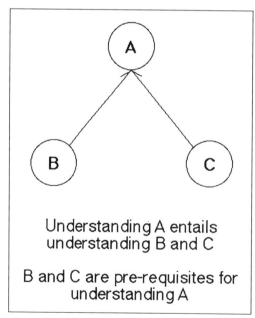

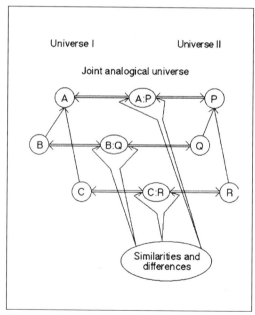

*Figure 4. A simple entailment structure.*

*Figure 5. An entailment structure with two analogous subject areas (universe of discourse).*

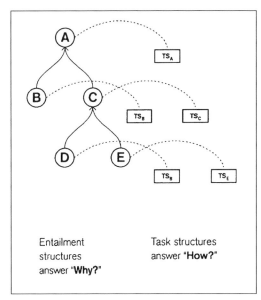

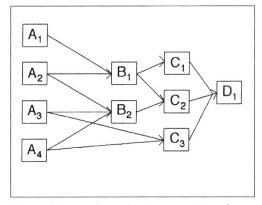

Figure 6. Entailment structure showing links to task structures.

analogy and using that as the basis for learning about the second universe, in this case universe 2.

Entailment structures reveal the *why* of knowledge, the conceptual structures that relate topics one to another. For a full semantics, the content of topics, their *how*, needs to be specified. This can be done operationally in the form of task structures, defined with respect to a canonical universe of discourse or modelling facility. In Pask's phrase, task structures show 'what may be done', they show the procedural knowledge or performative competencies that someone who understands a particular topic is deemed to have (See Figure 6).

Task structures may be represented in a variety of ways, for example, as a precedence chart showing order relations between the goals and sub-goals of a task (See Figure 7) or as a flow chart showing a sequence of operations, tests, branches and iterations (a simple example is shown in Figure 8).

We shall now extend the entailment structure representation of relations between topics in order to encompass the idea of coherence in a conceptual system and to capture the idea of a body of knowledge being a learnable, memorable whole. Essentially we can extend or elaborate entailment structures in four ways.

First, we can extend by analogy as already indicated in Figure 5. However, it should be appreciated that for analogy relations to be well defined there must be some sense in which the bodies of knowledge they are relating together are themselves coherent wholes.

Second, 'local cyclicity' can be introduced. This captures the idea that topics can be explained in terms of each other in different ways. Once topic A in Figure 4 is understood, topic B can be explained in terms of topics A and C and topic C can be explained in terms of topics A and B. These possibilities are shown in Figure 9 and Figure 10. When cyclicity is introduced into an entailment structure, Pask refers to the resulting form as an *entailment mesh*.

Figure 7. A precedence chart representation of a task structure.

17

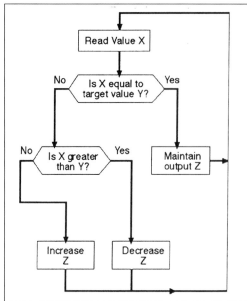

*Figure 8. A flow chart representation of a task structure (the example is a simple control process for maintaining the value of variable Z as a function of input variable X with a target value Y).*

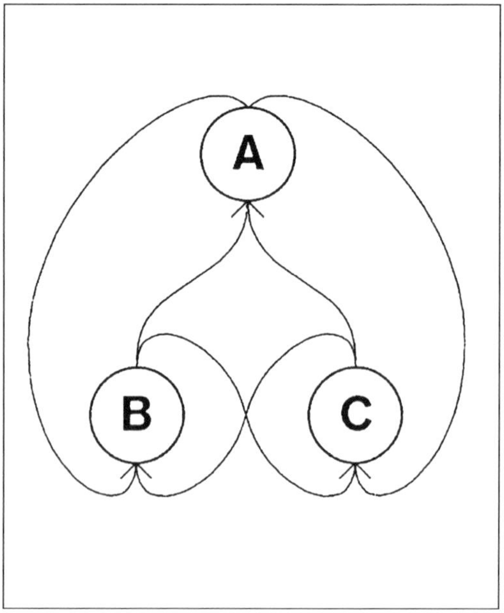

*Figure 9. Local cyclicity added to a small fragment of an entailment structure.*

Third, topics within an entailment structure or mesh may be 'unzipped', that is, analysed further in order to reveal sub-topics. For example, the topic 'table' may be unzipped to reveal subtopics concerned with 'having legs' or 'having a flat surface' .

Fourth, an entailment structure or mesh fragment may be embedded within a larger hierarchical form. For example, topics to do with 'furniture' may be embedded within a larger structure of topics concerned with 'human dwellings'. The operations of unzipping and embedding are depicted in Figure 11.

We arrive at the concept of coherence by modelling organisational closure within a system of concepts.

Strawson (1992) expresses the general idea thus:

> Let us imagine ... the model of an elaborate network, a system, of connected items, concepts, such that the function of ... each concept could ... be properly understood only by grasping its connections with the others, its place in the system ... there will be no reason to worry if, in the process of tracing connections from one point to another of the network, we find ourselves returning to our starting point .... the general charge of circularity would lose its sting for we might have moved in a wide, revealing, and illuminating circle.

We can model organisational closure as follows. Imagine that the edges of the

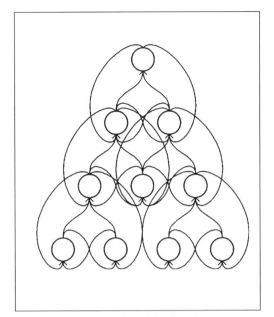

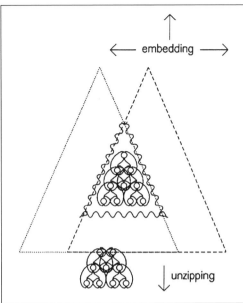

*Figure 10. Local cyclicity added for a larger fragment of an entailment structure.*

*Figure 11. Embedding and unzipping an entailment structure to form larger structures.*

entailment structure extend until they meet, as in Figure 12. Where the meeting of opposing edges, top and bottom, left and right results in a torus (Figure 13). Pask refers to this model of an organisationally closed systems of concepts as a 'globally cyclic' entailment mesh.

Having modelled conceptual coherence as a globally cyclic entailment mesh, we can now retrace our steps in order to articulate the concept of a narrative structure and to reveal the set of possible narrative structures that a particular knowledge structure may engender.

## 2.4 Constructing an expository narrative

For present purposes, a composer of an expository narrative is taken to be someone whose conceptual repertoire includes a coherent, stable conceptual system for the subject matter in question. We thus avoid considering the case where, in the act of composition, new understandings evolve. This simplifies the task of modelling narrative structures but, of course does not do full justice to the reality of composition. In Pask's writings, it is axiomatic that conceptual systems evolve, that 'man is a system that needs to learn' (Pask, 1968).

As above, we may model a conceptual system as an entailment mesh. The first step of composition then becomes that of 'adopting a perspective', assuming a point of view. Adopting a perspective on an entailment mesh has two complementary aspects, corresponding to the complementary processes of comprehension learning and operation learning referred to earlier:

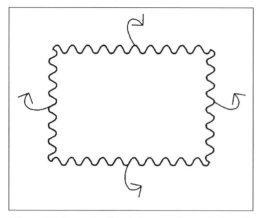

*Figure 12. Organisational closure of an entailment mesh.*

*Figure 13. A globally cyclic entailment mesh represented as a torus.*

- a head topic is distinguished with a supporting set of subordinate, entailed topics that are its conceptual support and justification from that perspective. In essence this corresponds to the act of isolating a hierarchical entailment structure from the entailment mesh in which it is embedded. Pask refers to this operation as 'pruning'. The only cyclic connections permitted in a pruned structure are those that relate two or more simple structures analogically (as in Figure 5);
- in principle and, at least, potentially, the adoption of a perspective calls forth one or more particular universes of discourse, which can be conceived of as multi-dimensional 'spaces' in which possible relations may be recognised, constructed and maintained. As earlier, Pask's generic term for a canonical version of such universes is 'modelling facility'.

Where the topic hierarchy is a simple entailment structure with one head topic and where the context does indeed serve as a universe of discourse that supports the permitted operations on relations, then the topic hierarchy may, by a suitable semantic, be placed in one to one correspondence with the task structures that operationally specify the content of those topics. That is, in general, where concepts are executable as operations, there is an isomorphism between the declarative aspects of conceptualisation concerned with saying *why* something is what it is, and the procedural aspects of conceptualisation concerned with saying *how* operations are carried out, how the concepts may be modelled or instantiated as relations in a particular context (modelling facility or universe).

The combination of conceptual coherence with executability of operations as the basis for an epistemology or model of knowledge is not peculiar to Pask, although he perhaps has developed the most detailed models. Rescher (1973, 1977) refers to 'conceptual idealism' combined with a 'methodological pragmatism'. George (1973) succinctly states that 'a theory is a model together with its interpretation'. Miller and

Johnson-Laird (1976) propose 'a conceptual theory of meaning … tied to procedural interpretation of sentences'.

Particular narratives composed may have different emphases, depending on the narrators' aims. Where there is an emphasis on teaching the *how* of operational content, as when teaching mastery of a set of skills, a clear mapping between topic descriptions (minimally, topic names) and particular operations is of signal importance. In military operations, such as dismantling an automatic weapon, there is a requirement to be able to 'name parts' but the emphasis is on being able to carry out operations.

Where the emphasis is on conceptual descriptions and *why* type explanations, task structures may be less well defined. They may even be a tacit assumption that the student is already familiar with the basic operational topology of the universe that is being talked about, so that they have the required set of operators to model and instantiate topics if so required. In this latter case it is not usual to insist on making explicit the isomorphism between entailment structure explanations and task structure operations. An example of this would be a lesson about the social consequences of genetic engineering, where a basic understanding of genetics is assumed.

Analogies may be thought of as topics which say how one set of topics may be transformed into another set of topics or, equivalently, as meta-narratives that say how one narrative may be transformed into or derived from another. When expounding analogies, different narrative sequences may be adopted depending on the students' needs and the demands of the subject matter being expounded. For example, one may set up a framework of correspondences of description saying that topics in one universe are indeed similar to another and, at a later stage, demonstrate this by matching operations and clarifying and highlighting by demonstration just what are the similarities and the differences between the topics in the two universes of discourse. Alternatively, one may provide operational experience and conceptual description in the two distinct contexts and establish the analogy relations at a later date. Indeed, part of a teaching strategy might be that one gives the learner the opportunity to recognise and establish those relations himself, by a process of what Spearman (1923) refers to as *eduction* (see Mason, 1994, for recent studies of the role of analogies in conceptual change).

## 2.5. Summary of the variety of forms of expository narrative

Here we look in more detail at just what are the various forms of expository narrative that a particular knowledge structure may engender.

First, notice that our exposition could well begin with an 'advance organiser' (Ausubel, 1968), preparing the student for what is to come. This is an optional but arguably very important part of an expository narrative if only for some learners, those whose learning style is biased towards global integration (see Pask and Scott, 1972). An expository narrative may also conclude with a summary or review of what was taught. Throughout the narrative structure, cross referencing may be deployed. What is in mind here is the teachers' dictum 'First say what is to be taught, then teach, then say what was taught'. This dictum may be applied and reapplied at different levels of resolution - for the subject matter as a whole and for particular topics and groups of topics within it.

An advance organiser might be a piece of text or a combination of graphics and text, for example, a concept map with descriptive labels. Typically, advance organisers are intended to convey something such as: 'This lesson is about topic A; in order to fully understand topic A, you need to first study topics B and C and then understand how they can be related together as an explanation or justification for topic A'. The advance organiser might also include information about sequencing, for example, 'First we will study topic B, then topic C, then topic A'.

Let us now consider the variety of narrative forms that might be constructed for the body of a lesson, accepting that advance organisers and summaries are optional 'add-ons'.

For each topic, there is a description of a 'rule'. There is also operational content to be demonstrated or ostended. In the simplest case, this consists of one or more examples of the rule at work.

The teaching sequence for a particular topic could take either the form of 'This is the rule, these are the examples' or 'These are some of the examples, this is the rule' (see Rowntree, 1990).

Critically, the rule for the head topic, topic A, explains why it is and what it is, in terms of the rules of topics B and C. Operationally, the instantiation of topic A includes the construction of forms, relations within which instantiations of B and C may be distinguished. The body of the narrative is then the chosen teaching sequence. It should be noted, however, that in tutorial conversation, where the teacher may be a human or a computer-based 'intelligent tutor', the actual teaching sequence followed may be a result of negotiation. That is, the learner may be permitted some degree of selection regarding the order of presentation of rules and demonstrations.

These considerations reveal that even a simple entailment structure may be the basis for a rich variety of narrative structures. As examples, Figure 14 shows a variety of forms of *why* narrative for just three related topics; Figure 15 shows the forms of *how* narrative where one of the three topics, as the head topic, is the goal of modelling operations in a modelling facility and finally, Figure 16 shows just some of the sequences whereby *how* and *why* aspects may be composed together. The reader is invited to contemplate the variety of narrative structures available for richer, more elaborate structures, involving analogies, analogies between analogies, meta-narratives and meta-meta-narratives.

## 2.6 Implications for computer-mediated communication

Pask's conversation theory (CT) has provided us with a useful model for the structure of knowledge, which in turn has helped reveal the large variety of forms that narratives about a particular body of knowledge may take. The model is particularly relevant for course design and communication in a hypertext environment. CT was used in the course design of the CASTE hypertext teaching environment and could clearly be applied to the authoring of hypertext-based courses for delivery over the

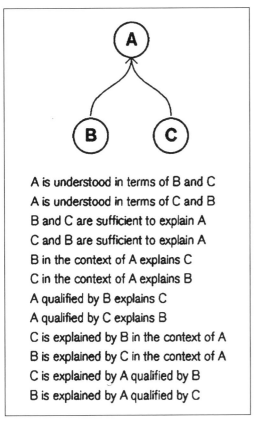

A is understood in terms of B and C
A is understood in terms of C and B
B and C are sufficient to explain A
C and B are sufficient to explain A
B in the context of A explains C
C in the context of A explains B
A qualified by B explains C
A qualified by C explains B
C is explained by B in the context of A
B is explained by C in the context of A
C is explained by A qualified by B
B is explained by A qualified by C

*Figure 14. Forms of 'why' narrative.*

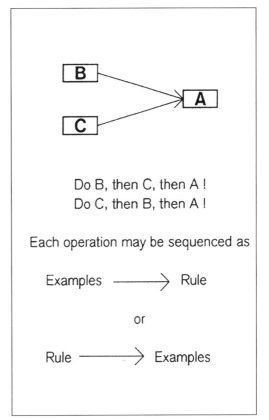

Do B, then C, then A !
Do C, then B, then A !

Each operation may be sequenced as

Examples ⟶ Rule

or

Rule ⟶ Examples

*Figure 15. Forms of 'how' narrative.*

World Wide Web. CT provides a well-tried methodology for knowledge and task analysis and a transparent, pedagogically-sound semantics for classifying types of hypertext link (Scott, 1998). [Editors' note: CT modelling therefore offers a principled approach to addressing some of the concerns expressed by Henriquez, in Chapter 1 of this volume, over the uncertainty engendered by the lack of semantically typed hypertext links as they are implemented in the WWW.]

## 2.7 Concluding Remarks

Space has limited our attention to the structure of expository narratives. Pask himself was fascinated by the structure of dramas and how to represent characters as roles (see Pask, 1976, Chapter 10). Pask was also fascinated by the dynamics of mental life and conceptualisation. The account given here of narrative composition and entailment meshes may be interpreted as a series of static snapshots of activities within a dynamical self-organising, self-reproducing system of concepts. Such a system learns by evolving and becoming more informed, but it is also constrained to maintain a focus of attention, to survive as a centre of awareness. In doing so, it becomes informed about itself.  Pask was also fascinated by conversation - how persons, as p-individuals, converse or exchange stories with others and with themselves. He was particularly motivated to promote the understanding that the right kind of story-telling is that which promotes the freedom to be different and individual while conserving the unity of love and mutual respect (Pask, 1990). Knowledge elicitation and modelling methodologies

"Why?" of A is explained in terms of B and C

Possible sequences

Explain A → Explain B → Do B → Explain C → Do C → Do A

Do B → Explain B → Do C → Explain C → Do A → Explain A

*Figure 16. Forms of narrative combining 'how' with 'why'.*

may usefully serve to help ensure participants in conversation do understand each other, even though they may agree to disagree about the 'truth' of particular knowledge content.

## Acknowledgement

I wish to thank my colleague, Steve Ryan, for his support and helpful suggestions during the writing of this chapter.

# 3. Anchors in Context: a corpus analysis of authoring conventions for web pages

Einat Amitay

## 3.1 Introduction

The study of text and its linguistic characteristics - syntactic structure, use of discourse context, lexical choice, page layout - is one which is interesting both to descriptive linguists and to computational linguists designing systems to generate human-like texts. The linguistic characteristics of the web page, a very new phenomenon, are, naturally enough, much less extensively described and well understood than those of other, longer-standing genres and media. The current study aims at identifying some of these emerging linguistic characteristics of World Wide Web pages.

The particular focus of the study will be the text used to label hypertext links at their anchor points. This is a little-studied topic - studies such as McDonald and Stevenson (1996; 1997) and Wright (1993) have focused on the text within a node, but not the content of the link labels. Link labelling would appear at first sight to be eminently worth studying as it is closely related to at least two problems which Conklin identified in his pioneering analysis, i.e. the 'lost in hyperspace' phenomenon, where the reader feels lost in a over-abundance of unstructured information, and the 'cognitive overload' phenomenon, where the reader is forced to spend cognitive resources on managing their reading strategies, rather than processing content (Conklin, 1987).

## 3.2 Methodology

A corpus of web pages was collected and the linguistic features of the anchor text appearing on the pages were analysed. The Home Corpus comprises 155 HTML files and is a collection of personal home-pages submitted after a request to several mailing lists and newsgroups. These will obviously be a self-selecting sample, rather than a random one, and their nature will be determined by the mail lists and newsgroups on which the request for participation was posted. However, we believe they serve their purpose of furnishing a wide range of personal home pages for study.

## 3.3 Analysing the Home Corpus

The content of the hypertext documents was studied through a statistical analysis of the words which comprise the HTML files of the Home Corpus. They were divided into two groups:

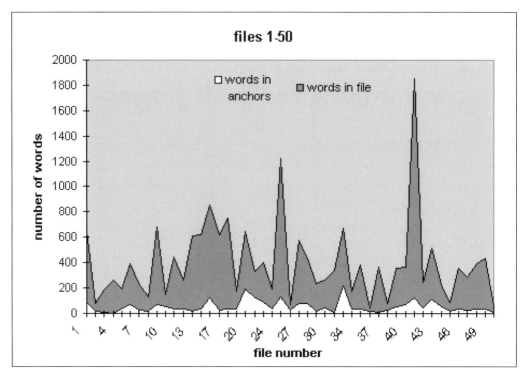

*Figure 1.*

## Group One

The words which appear on the screen (excluding, for technical reasons, the words which appear in image form). Total number of words: 48,963

## Group Two

The words (a subset of Group One) which form the anchors. Total number of words: 7391.

### *Anchor text to other text ratio*

The ratio between total number of words and words in anchors for each file was calculated. The ratio between all the words in the file (grey) and the words in the anchors (white) is shown for each file from 001.html -100.html in Figure 1 and Figure 2.

The graph shows for some of the files an increase in the number of words used as anchors as the number of words per file increases. However this is only a local tendency and is not linearly proportionate with the number of words. This is an interesting finding because it means that the length of the document does not directly dictate the number of links, which might have seemed a plausible hypothesis.

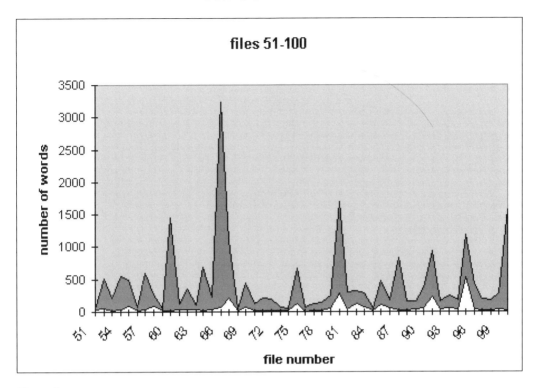

*Figure 2.*

## General linguistic features of hypertext documents

Two approaches were taken to studying the general linguistic features of the pages of the corpus. The first involved analysing frequency lists of words from both the anchor and other words in the files. The second is a detailed study of examples from the Home Corpus.

Table 1 is a frequency list of words which appear throughout the Home Corpus files, i.e. not simply the anchor text. The list shows the top 35 words.

The personal voice people use in writing hypertext is one interesting observation emerging from this list. Since the Home Corpus is a collection of personal home-pages it is not surprising that first person forms would be very high in the list. However the second person pronoun is also placed very high, indicating a tendency to use direct, situated and informal language - from me [the author] to you [the reader].

The authors of the Home Corpus seem to have a fairly homogeneous set of interests, with 'research', 'university' and 'language' appearing high on the list. 'Language' could denote a computing as well as a linguistic orientation, and 'information', while possibly suggesting an academic environment, could also simply be part of the hypertext environment where the authors supply a link to more information on the subject discussed.

The other words in the list are mainly function words. A comparison with the top 35

| 2215 | the | | 281 | you | | 177 | that |
|------|-----|--|-----|-----|--|-----|------|
| 1633 | of | | 277 | this | | 177 | have |
| 1335 | and | | 266 | with | | 176 | research |
| 1003 | in | | 231 | university | | 165 | m |
| 957 | a | | 231 | page | | 165 | be |
| 922 | to | | 220 | are | | 161 | here |
| 627 | i | | 205 | from | | 158 | or |
| 518 | is | | 204 | by | | 149 | home |
| 409 | on | | 194 | an | | 139 | information |
| 362 | my | | 192 | it | | 130 | me |
| 331 | s | | 190 | language | | | |
| 303 | at | | 185 | as | | | |

*Table 1. Top 35 lexical items.*

words of a frequency list taken from the British National Corpus (BNC), which includes 100,000,000 words, shows the similarities and dissimilarities shown in Table 2.

There are 10 items in each list which do not appear in the other. For the BNC the items can be divided into four groups:
• 'was' and 'had', which relate to tense and aspect;
• 'he', 'his', 'they', 'she' and 'we', which relate to person;
• 'but' and 'which',  coherence related items;
• 'not'.

The BNC frequency list contains all the tense variations for the verbs 'to have' and 'to be' (with the sole exception of 'am'), while the Home corpus frequency list includes only the present tense of these verbs. This suggests that there is a strong preference for using the present tense in writing home-pages. Since home-pages are collections of persistent facts about people, it is perhaps not surprising to find that the tense used for writing them is the present. The fact that web pages are relatively easy to update may also be a factor here.

The fact that there are no third person animate pronouns in the Home Corpus top 35 frequency list suggests that a 'conversational' tone in the home pages, with interaction between the author, writing in the first person singular, and the reader, referred to in the second person.

In general writing, the words 'but' and 'which' are used mostly to connect two clauses, to create a longer, more complex sentence, or to expand the context of a noun phrase, again, raising its internal complexity.  From the absence of these words from the corpus we can infer that people tend to write short, simple sentences on their home pages, avoiding more complex structures which would involve greater processing effort from readers and run the risk of misunderstandings and ambiguities. The word 'and', however, is less problematic to process and is used on home pages as a connective between two simple sentences, noun phrases and so on.

| | | | |
|---|---|---|---|
| 2215 the | 220 are | 6187925 the | 517783 as |
| 1633 of | 205 from | 2941786 of | 513075 by |
| 1335 and | 204 by | 2682874 and | 478177 at |
| 1003 in | 194 an | 2560344 to | 473691 have |
| 957 a | 192 it | 2150872 a | 470949 are |
| 922 to | 190 language | 1883290 in | 463235 this |
| 627 i | 185 as | 1115377 that | 462776 not |
| 518 for | 177 that | 1089558 it | 456071 but |
| 459 is | 177 have | 998857 is | 445396 had |
| 409 on | 176 research | 923972 was | 433594 his |
| 362 my | 165 m | 905318 i | 433475 they |
| 331 s | 165 be | 851722 for | 413532 from |
| 303 at | 161 here | 807305 's | 380284 she |
| 281 you | 158 or | 724195 on | 372031 which |
| 277 this | 149 home | 695595 you | 370855 or |
| 266 with | 139 information | 681374 he | 358792 we |
| 231 university | 130 me | 664778 be | 344045 an |
| 231 page | | 652050 with | |
| Home Corpus | | British National Corpus | |

*Table 2. Top 35 words from Home and British National Corpora.*

We would suggest two possible explanations for the absence of 'not'. The first is that the informal style adopted by home page authors would lead them to choose the contracted form of negative verb forms (can't, won't, don't and so on) rather than the full form. In addition, it may also run counter to the straightforward 'setting out the facts' perspective that people want to create.

From the 10 words which appear in the Home Corpus top 35 frequency list and not in the BNC list we can learn more about the stylistic preferences of the authors of the hypertext documents. These 10 words can also be divided into groups:

• the first group includes the words 'my', 'm' (found in the contracted form 'I'm') and 'me'. The existence of this group reinforces the claim made earlier that the language used on home pages tends to be direct and informal;

• the second group consists of 'university' and 'research', strong indicators of the content of the Home Corpus: it is a collection of home pages of people who work in universities and are involved in research;

• the third group is made up of 'language' and 'information' which can be associated with both the content of the documents (research and universities), and with home pages and hypertext;

• the final group of words is 'page', 'here' and 'home', whose use is in part at least a reflection of the tendency to conceptualise a home page in spatial terms, as a 'place' in hyperspace.

This last group is particularly interesting when viewed in the context of word pairs or bigrams found most frequently within the Home Corpus. These are as shown in Table 3.

The words 'home' and 'page' often appear juxtaposed (231 occurrences of 'page', 149 occurrences of 'home', 105 occurrences of 'home page'). However, the word 'page' appears more than 50 per cent of the time without 'home'. However, when it does occur, it substitutes semantically for 'home page'.

The word 'here' appears to be also a part of a regular pair, i.e. 'click here' (161 occurrences of 'here', 65 occurrences of 'click', 49 occurrences of 'click here'). This combination is unique to the environment of web navigation. A very interesting behaviour of this combination can be found by looking at their positions in the bigram and monogram frequency list in the *anchors* of the Home Corpus: only 16 'click here' bigrams but 82 occurrences of 'here' in different linguistic contexts. The word 'here' also appears as a one-word-anchor 60 times, i.e. in 73 per cent of its occurrences in anchor text. This strongly indicates that is it used not only as a spatial indicator but also as an imperative instruction, much as an interaction icon.

Such directional instructions given by authors are unique to hypertext - it is unlikely and unconventional to find an author of 'flat' text telling readers to turn the page. This active, guiding rôle is taken on because authors no longer count on verbal cues and linguistic conventions to guide their readers, but also add explicit physical instructions to control their readers' behaviour. Charney (1994) suggests a need for authors to assume this rôle:

> .. for readers to make appropriate connections between related ideas, the sentences expressing these ideas should appear in close proximity. Thus a text is easier to read if its points are developed in coherent sequences of sentences, paragraphs, and sections and if it contains discourse cues that signal the relations among these ideas.... Since readers use high-level ideas to tie portions of text together, these concepts should be explicitly stated early in the text and should be clearly signalled so that the reader can easily recall them as the need arises.... Thus it is easier to read, comprehend, and remember a text if it contains an informative title, headings, overviews, and topic sentences introducing key concepts that are repeated and developed in successive portions of text....These strategies, however, place the burden of selecting and arranging information, and providing signals to the arrangement, primarily on the writer. Hypertexts, by shifting a large portion of this burden to the reader, by proliferating the readers' choices about what portions of a text to read and in what order, compound the difficulties of creating a coherent mental representation.

Whalley (1993) suggests that we can place different types of reader-author relations on a continuum, with genres such as the course reader or distance learning text characterised by a great deal of cohesive reference, at the 'author control' end of the scale, and hypertext-like works such as encyclopaedias and reference manuals characterised by little cohesive reference, at the 'reader control' end. He also suggests that 'the amorphous 'links' provided by hypertext do not provide any true cohesive

| |
|---|
| of the |
| in the |
| university of |
| at the |
| on the |
| home page |
| I am |
| to the |
| department of |
| for the |
| and the |
| is a |
| from the |
| the university |
| natural language |
| if you |
| cognitive science |
| to be |
| I have |
| of my |
| click here |

*Table 3. Most frequent bigrams*

reference. If everything is related to everything then essentially no cohesion is provided'.

These two researchers pinpoint the reason for inserting more physical instruction into the body of hypertext. These verbal directions as to where the reader should go from a certain point in the text are part of the convention of writing hypertext documents, probably because people find that there is a need for more guidance in reading such a spatially complex text. All the phenomena studied in the above paragraphs seem to indicate that authors do their best to facilitate their readers' experience of their pages. They use direct and informal language. They avoid complex linguistic structures. They use the present tense, avoiding negatives and counterfactuals. They treat the page as a physical space and suggest that that the document is in the here and now. Above all they try to assist the readers by supplying them with guidelines on how to read their pages.

## The unique function of determiners in hypertext

Conventional discourse genres can be ascribed a beginning, a body and an end. Even an informal conversation exhibits typical opening and closing events. However, it is much less straightforward to define the beginning and end of a hypertext document, unless it consists of a single page.

When we take a book from the shelf and start reading it, we can always 'jump' to its end to see what has become of the hero, or what the answer to the riddle is, but after doing that we know that there is no other end to this book. Even if we keep on reading from where we were before, the end will remain the same, and in the identical place it was before. In other words, the size and content of the text would remain the same. In hypertext the dimensions of the total context are not defined since the links are part of the hypertext which makes up the World Wide Web and may lead to other documents with links which lead to yet other documents and so on, effectively ad infinitum. A 'flat' text thus has a textual integrity which hypertexts lack. As Landow (1992) says:

electronic linking … disperses 'the' text into other texts. As an individual lexia loses its physical and intellectual separation from others when linked electronically to them, it finds itself dispersed into them. The necessary contextuality and intertextuality produced

31

by situating individual reading units within a network of easily navigable pathways weaves texts, including those by different authors and those in non-verbal media, tightly together. One effect of this process is to weaken and perhaps destroy any sense of textual uniqueness (p.53; see also pages 57-59).

One way hypertext authors can minimise the possible confusion of readers in this multiplicity of documents is to use definite and indefinite articles  to make explicit what the reader ought to assume as basic world knowledge and what they are not

*Table 4.*

| | |
|---|---|
| The (almost) Complete Guide to WWW in Israel | The Goodies |
| The Adaptive Hypertext and Hypermedia Homepage | The Guardian newspaper on-line |
| | The Hazardous Materials Sheet for Women |
| The Argus Clearing House | The HCI Research school in Stockholm |
| The Back 40: Archaeology | The history of king Richard the Thirde |
| The Beggar's Opera | The "home page" of my thesis |
| The Book of the Courtier | The "homeopathic fallacy" in learning from hypertext" |
| The Brown University Home Page | |
| The Center For Cognitive Science | The HPSG Workshop |
| The Centre for the Easily Amused (C*E*A) | The Humanist Web |
| The Chesapeake Bay Bolide: | The Integration of AM/FM and Work Management |
| The Chronicles of England | |
| The Clickable Anthony | The Interdisciplinary Weekly Tea Seminar |
| The Coconut Veranda | The Irish Chess Archive |
| The comp.fonts Home Page | The Java programming Language |
| The Data Mine | The Java Repository |
| The Day the Universe Went All Funny: | The JRR Tolkien  Information Page- Info about my favorite author. |
| The Duke of Edinburgh's Award International Association | |
| | The Koine Greek Verb: Tense and Aspect. |
| The Dukes of Hazzard. Yeeha! | The Korin Richmond Repository. |
| The Electronic Neanderthal Woodworker | The Lady of May |
| The Electrotechnical Laboratory | The Language Software Helpdesk |
| The English-Norwegian parallel corpus project | The Language Software Helpdesk |
| The Faerie Queene | The Language Technology Group |
| The Fine Print | The last of the greats - Alice and Peter's 50th Birthday Party |
| The Fortune 500 firms, 1996 | |
| The Fountain of Moravec | The Legal Stuff (how you can/cannot use this) |
| The Fowre Hymnes | The LINGUIST Network |
| The Free On-line Dictionary of Computing | The Living  Room: HOT LINKS |
| The Gaelic college | The LTG crew |
| The Garden of the World Project | The lunar calendar of Tablet  Mamari", Journal de la |
| The Geological Society of America | |
| The Gernsback Continuum | The MainStay BBS ADDRESS BOOK |

expected to know. Akmajian *et al.* (1995) describe the rôle of definite and indefinite articles as the indicating cues for presuppositions and given-new information. Since a single hypertext document can be accessed from many directions, authors tend to introduce information in a very cautious way, using determiners to characterise the information given, and to let the reader know the immediate context of this information.

Let us examine the occurrence of the definite article in anchors. Table 4 includes all the anchors in the Home Corpus which begin with the definite article. This list consists

*Table 4 (cont.).*

| |
|---|
| The Mammoth Saga |
| The Migraine Project |
| The Modern English Collection |
| The Music Room: Claire & Her Music. |
| The Natural Language Processing Group in the Department of AI. |
| The Net, BBC TV |
| The New Age |
| The NLP Software Registry Homepage |
| The normal home page - only for local users |
| The Official Homepage of Toad The Wet Sprocket- one of the best bands ever! |
| The Pearl Dive |
| The Pixel Forge: Hand Hammered Special Effects (slow load; lotta pictures) |
| The Poetry Corner |
| The Press Room: Media lies and distortions. NEW!!! |
| The Program, ITV |
| The Sacred Chao |
| The Sacred Chao |
| The Scotland index |
| The Semantics and Pragmatics of Lexical Aspect Features. |
| The SFEP-ED-L homepage |
| The Shepheardes Calender |
| The Simpsons; |
| The Sinclair Archive |
| The Sinclair ZX Spectrum Switchboard |
| The Skylight: Life On Mars? |
| The Spam Filter |
| The Sunsite Gaelic homepage |
| The Syntax and Semantics of Predication |

| |
|---|
| The Tony Godwin Memorial Trust homepage |
| The Tree of Life Home Page |
| The University of Berkeley Museum of Paleontology |
| The University of Cambridge |
| The University of Edinburgh |
| The Unofficial Haitian Home Page |
| The Vicarious Learner Project |
| The Virtual Earth |
| The Voyager CD-Rom |
| The Windows 95 FAQs |
| The WWW Virtual Library |
| The WWW Virtual Library |
| The WWW yellow pages of Israel |
| The Zero Point Knowledge Unit |
| the author's page here |
| the Centre for Cognitive Science |
| the DEFACTO project |
| the Department of AI |
| the DRAFTER project |
| the GIST project |
| the Human Communication Research Centre |
| the list of publications |
| the NLP group |
| the release announcement |
| the University of Edinburgh |
| the webmaster |

mostly of noun phrases which are preceded by the definite article. The definite article is capitalised in most anchors and refers to an external existing object. This is slightly surprising since conventionally the definite article introduces given knowledge, yet in these cases, an unknown and new quantity is being introduced. These anchors appear to be token-reflexive (Reichenbach, 1947; Burks, 1949; Sellars, 1956). Token-reflexive expressions are expressions which serve to connect the circumstances in which a statement is made with its sense. Such a definition would help in explaining why people use the definite article when they refer to external and previously unseen or unmentioned objects. The additional information provided by the use of the definite article is a valuable one. It means that in the local context there is only one object by that name and that this is a fact known to the author. It also coins a new term or proper name to be used in this given environment, in order to use it as a 'verbal button'. Sellars (1956) claims, in the context of basic world knowledge and conversation, that such token-reflexive expressions add both authority and credibility to the text. The text becomes more authoritative because the author's assertions are definitive and therefore assumed to be true. Inserting new knowledge, presented as if it was known to both the author and the reader, contributes to the factual environment people want to create in their web pages.

On the other hand, authors tend to use the *indefinite* article to stress that the links given are only a sample from what might be a large collection of occurrences of similar documents or sites, as in the following examples:

- A Japanese Easter Island site
- A clickable map of Wales
- A clue
- A cool trivia page
- A corpus for teaching Portuguese
- A map of Israel & its neighbouring states
- A page dedicated to my second favorite author: David Eddings
- A picture of Bangor

## 3.4 Conclusions

The linguistic devices used in hypertext can thus be explained in the following way. Authors introduce themselves and their environment to the reader, describing the context of their document with the most explicit information, giving name, place and sometime even date. This well-described context allows them to refer to their document as being here and other hypertext documents as being there or elsewhere. When the author wants to introduce new information, or refer to an outside document they simply assert its existence by naming it and thus defining and inserting new facts into the document. The only knowledge needed in order to navigate between documents, then, is the understanding that each hypertext document has a local environment and if the reader wants to know more about one of the facts introduced by the author, all they have to do is click this new fact and jump to its local environment. Of course such a jump might show the fact and its explained context but it would probably introduce more factual objects in the new local context. Action words such as 'here', 'this', 'back to' and 'home page', within the hypertext writing convention, act as cues and road signs as to where a starting point can be found. These words appear to be used in similar contexts and syntactic structure, facilitating orientation within and between documents.

This illustration of the hypertext document local context can also support and explain the findings, retrieved from the Home Corpus, that there is no proportion between the length of documents and the number of links they contain - too many unfamiliar objects in one local context can create distraction and incoherent text (Charney, 1994). Since the local environment of hypertext documents appears to be the whole HTML file, the number of new inserted linked-objects is limited within their physical surroundings. It seems that the structure of paragraphs has no affect on the number of inserted links and that the latter is restricted to fit coherence limitations. Although it can sometimes seem that there is no real order and method in writing hypertext documents, the findings in this chapter suggest that there are pragmatic reasons for the consistent choices made by hypertext authors in their use of a wide range of linguistic devices.

# 4. Scholarly Email Discussion List Postings: a single new genre of academic communication?

Helmut Gruber

## 4.1 Introduction

Present day computer technology offers a wide variety of synchronous and asynchronous forms of computer-mediated communication (CMC). One question which arises in this context is whether each (technologically defined) different form of CMC has to be viewed as a communicative genre of its own or if within a single mode of CMC different linguistic genres may be found.

In a comprehensive quantitative study, Yates compared CMC data from email conference systems with written and spoken data-samples (Yates, 1996). His results seem to indicate that email communication displays linguistic properties which set it apart from both written and spoken modes of communication. However, Yates and Graddol (1996), examining different kinds of CMC such as video-conferencing, Internet Relay Chat (IRC) and conference system data, show that CMC cannot be viewed as a single genre but must be divided into several distinctive forms of communication. Cho's (1996) study of email communication in an administrative setting indicates that despite some shared linguistic features between messages, there is also considerable individual variance between messages of the same type of CMC. Cho attributes this inter-individual variance to the fact that no stable genre expectations have yet been developed by email users.

This chapter presents some results of a study on email communication in scholarly discussion lists, which establish a new form of academic discussion (1). I apply a combination of quantitative and qualitative discourse analytic methods to investigate whether discussion list communication can be viewed as a single communicative genre or if even in this limited domain of CMC different subgenres have yet evolved.

## 4.2 Theoretical background: do list contributions establish a genre?

In his approach to academic genres, Swales (1990) postulates a strong relationship between 'discourse communities' and 'genres'. Applying the criteria he presents to define discourse communities to characterise the subscribers of academic discussion lists, it seems quite obvious to view them as discourse communities according to five of Swales' six features, because:

- both discussion lists under investigation have 'a broadly agreed set of common public goals' (Swales, 1990, p. 24);
- they have 'mechanisms of intercommunication among (their) members' (Swales, 1990, p. 25), namely the many-to-many communication mode of the Listserv-software;
- they use their 'participatory mechanisms primarily to provide information and feedback' (Swales, 1990, p. 26);
- they have 'acquired a specific lexis' (Swales, 1990, p. 26): on the LINGUIST list terminology from all areas of linguistics can be found, on the ETHNO list ethnomethodological and conversation analytic terminology prevails;
- they also have 'a threshold level of members with a suitable degree of relevant content and discoursal expertise' (Swales, 1990, p. 27): see the (infrequent) complaints of 'competent' subscribers about 'unnecessary' or even 'dumb' questions, which are posted on the lists sometimes.

The main question posed in this paper is whether there is a single genre which can be named 'scholarly email discussion list contribution' in the same sense as there is the genre 'scientific paper in the humanities and social sciences'. If this is the case, list subscribers would also meet Swales' sixth criterion for a discourse community, namely 'a discourse community utilizes and hence possesses one or more genres in the communicative furtherance of its aims' (Swales, 1990, p.26).

A look at Swales' defining features of genre (Swales, 1990, p. 45) seems to suggest a positive answer to this question, because:

- contributions to the lists are communicative events which are significantly influenced by technological possibilities and communicators' expectations;
- there seems to be a shared set of communicative purposes for discussion lists although there is some variation - according to an informal (and non-representative) survey which I conducted on the two lists, many list subscribers agree that discussing theoretical and/ or methodological problems is the main purpose and advantage of discussion lists (about 40 per cent), but there are also other communicative purposes such as obtaining information and references about certain subfields, etc.;
- there are constraints on what constitutes an appropriate contribution to a discussion which were explicitly verbalised on both lists during meta-discussions about the proper content of list contributions (i.e. should 'silly' or 'irrelevant' questions be forbidden in some way) and the proper way of quoting email contributions;
- at least on the LINGUIST there is discourse community's nomenclature for genres insofar as different content categories (like 'discussion', 'question', 'call for papers', 'jobs', etc.) exist.

Again, whether list postings also meet Swales' final criterion for genres (the 'prototypicality of contributions', Swales, 1990) is the central question of this paper. Thus, at first sight, list subscribers and their contributions seem to meet almost all of Swales' standards for discourse communities and genres.

However, a closer examination of Swales' approach raises a fundamental question - have subscribers of each discussion list to be viewed as one single discourse community or is there a general discourse community of 'list subscribers in the field of linguistics/discourse studies'? This question is not trivial because a positive answer would suggest that persons who subscribe to different discussion lists within one academic field would move between discourse communities every time they open their new-mail folder to read contributions to different lists, and, more relevantly, would have to apply different types of genre knowledge when reading and contributing messages. The results of the empirical study may provide an answer to this question.

## 4.3  Data and methodology

Discussions from two linguistic discussion lists, the LINGUIST and the ETHNO list, form the database of my study.

The LINGUIST list, as one of the oldest discussion lists in the area of linguistics, has several thousand subscribers and discussion topics are not restricted to a special sub-field of linguistics. It is a moderated list.

The ETHNO list is a non-moderated list, with discussion topics restricted to questions concerning ethnomethodology and conversation analysis. Conference announcements and calls for papers appear very rarely and there are no job announcements.

Three discussions in these two lists were systematically investigated on the textual and intertextual level and provided the main empirical basis of my study. The discussions took place during July and October 1995. Two of them  were conducted on the LINGUIST list (51 messages) and one on the ETHNO list (30 messages).

## 4.4  Results

### Spoken, written  or something else? Results of the quantitative analysis

It is a widespread view that email communication is a hybrid form of speech, situated somewhere between spoken and written discourse (Ferrara, Brunner and Whittemore, 1991; Ekhlund, 1986; Yates, 1996) (2). Therefore, in order to arrive at a first, rough and descriptive characterisation of the email messages under investigation I adopted some categories of Chafe and Danielewicz's (1987) investigation of differences between spoken and written academic discourse. Some  additional categories were added to account for characteristics of the data which seemed to be relevant.

In this step of the investigation, two discussions of my database were analysed, one from the LINGUIST list ('sex and language', 17 contributions), and one from the ETHNO list ('O.J. Simpson debate', 30 contributions). Table 1 provides an overview of the results. Numbers are either relative frequency counts, or else they show the frequency of the respective category per 1000 words. This measure was used for some categories to allow a direct comparison with Chafe and Danielewicz's results).

Because of space restrictions the comparison between Chafe and Danielewicz's (1987) results and the outcomes of this study have to be very short. At a rather superficial level of quantitative analysis it turns out that the only major difference between the texts of the two lists concerns the length of contributions, i.e. postings to the LINGUIST list are approximately twice as long as postings to the ETHNO list. In all other categories

|  | LD1 | ED1 | Total | C/D (1987) |  |
|---|---|---|---|---|---|
| type/ token ratio | 0.56 | 0.67 | 0.63 | 0.24 | (ap) |
| no. of clauses per contribution | 30.24 | 14.97 | 20.49 |  |  |
| words per clause | 15.41 | 16.07 | 15.83 | 9.30 | (ap) |
| no. of PPs per 1000words | 71.60 | 59.70 | 64.00 | 88.00 | (lc) |
| % of coordinated clauses | 17.11 | 13.37 | 14.73 | 12.00 | (lt) |
| % of subordinated clauses | 37.87 | 29.25 | 32.37 |  |  |
| no. of 1st pers. sg. pronouns per 1000 words | 21.40 | 21.00 | 21.20 | 21.00 | (lc) |
| academic hedges per 1000 words | 2.30 | 0.30 | 2.80 | 4.00 | (co) |
| expressions of personal beliefs: | 1.65 | 1.07 | 1.28 |  |  |
| **no. of references:** | **1.18** | **0.27** | **0.60** |  |  |
| personal experiences: | 0.59 | 0.30 | 0.40 |  |  |
| *question/ Answer structure:* | *1.12* | *1.33* | *1.26* |  |  |

LD1    LINGUIST discussion 1
ED1    ETHNO discussion 1
C/D    Chafe/ Danielewicz
ap     academic papers,
lt     letters
lc     lectures
co     conversations
**bold print:** indicators for "written language"
normal print: indicators for "spoken language"
*italics:* indicators for technological mode of communication

*Table 1. Categories/data set*

differences between the two lists were minimal. Thus, at this level it is possible to view the texts under consideration as belonging to one class.

A comparison with Chafe and Danielewicz's results shows that the postings cannot definitely be related to spoken or to written academic language exclusively. At the level of lexical variation, which is measured by type/token ratio, the degree of planning (words/clause) and the chaining of clauses (coordination vs. subordination), the texts can be compared to written academic papers or letters. On the other hand, looking at features like complexity or density of expression (measured by number of personal pronouns) and involvement with one's audience (use of first person singular pronouns) and the use of academic hedges (e.g. 'normally', 'usually') they resemble spoken language. Additionally, the results display striking similarities with the results of other quantitative investigations of CMC (Yates, 1996; Cho, 1996) which suggests that messages from asynchronous email communication have some features in common which distinguish them from other forms of spoken and written language.

A look at those categories which have no counterpart in the Chafe and Danielewicz study (or other studies of CMC), completes the picture.

Personal beliefs is a category similar to 'academic hedges' - it covers all instances where writers explicitly question or qualify their own assumptions or statements (for example, 'in my opinion'). Like the measures for academic hedges, 'personal beliefs' were expressed rather infrequently. The tendency to question or qualify one's own assumptions or point of view is higher in the LINGUIST than in the ETHNO list, although both counts are very low.

The number of references accounts for the fact that some authors in the discussions backed their claims and assertions by quoting literature. Obviously, this habit is adopted from writing academic papers. Again in the LINGUIST list the tendency to include references is higher than in the ETHNO list, but measures are generally low. Question-answer structure means that contributors may take a section from a previous contribution as 'questionable material' and comment on it in their own posting. Thus, this category covers a central feature of email communication that is normally referred to as 'quoting' (Du Bartell, 1995; Gruber, 1996a, 1996b). Its occurrence is a result of the technological component of the communication process, i.e. the fact that email software makes it quite simple to include earlier postings into a message. Results show that in both lists more than one explicit reference (with direct or indirect quotation) to a previous message is made. This means that thematic connections between postings are relatively tight in both lists.

Personal experience covers all instances of 'everyday narratives' which might be included in list-contributions. In all cases they are in some way related to the content of the current posting (and/or discussion), but their occurrence clearly shows that list postings are not only academic texts but also parts of 'everyday' interaction. Although the mean values of this category are quite low in both lists, the mere fact that this kind of discursive practice does occur shows that list contributors do not view email discussions exclusively as a scholarly activity but that they want to share their everyday experiences with others and contextualise the process of their thinking and working.

Generally, the quantitative results show that in almost all categories the differences between the two lists were minimal. Thus, these results would suggest that we view the texts under consideration as belonging to one class. However, the results of the qualitative analysis show a slightly different picture.

## Two modes of quoting

Once a new discussion topic has been established, any list subscriber may join a discussion. Turn-taking in the sense of Sacks, Schegloff and Jefferson (1974) does not take place because any 'speaker' may self-select him/herself at any time during a discussion.

Reference to (one or more) previous messages is one of the main features of (reactive) email messages in general, which is facilitated by the email software facility that allows a user to include and edit the message they are responding to. Two major types of back-reference were found - direct and indirect quoting.

The following extract is an example of an unprefaced overt disagreement with a previous posting using direct quoting:

### Extract 1:
```
'On the language/dialect discussion, AL2 [full name] says:
> Date:  Thu, 28 Sep 1995 16:35:00 PDT
> From:  AL2 [login name]
> Subject:  Disc 2 [original thread] more
>
>  ...
> A final thought on the above problem is that some people
> will argue on the basis of the standard that, say, there
> is no continuum between Spanish and Portuguese because
> "Spanish"means standard Spanish, also known by,
> the "dialectal" name castellano and Gallego, the Galician
> transition between Northern and Northern "Portuguese" is > a
separate language, not Spanish.
^^^^^^^^^^^
This is indeed an awkward formulation.  It presupposes, by
negation, that Galizan could be considered a dialect of
*Spanish*.  The use of the Spanish name "Gallego" for it, instead
of the native Portuguese term "Galego" or either of the English
translations Galician/Gallegan (both, by the way, derived from
Spanish "Galicia" and "gallego") reflects a dubiously informed
view about the nature of the native dialects of Galiza
Portuguese." (OL2, 6. Oct, LINGUIST-List, disc. 2)
```

Extract 1 represents the beginning of a rather long reactive contribution that is highly relevant for the current discussion. On the formal level it is an example of 'direct quoting', i.e. the inclusion of parts of a previous posting in the actual message. This practice of 'quoting' is often viewed as the only way in which email users refer to earlier contributions (see Wetzstein, 1995; DuBartell, 1995), yet we shall see that this is not true for the discussion lists under consideration. Direct quotes are marked off from the 'auctorial text' by means of an alphanumeric sign ('>') at the beginning of each quoted line. In this case the author quotes not only the portions of text he refers to and comments on but also the software-generated parts of the text, i.e. date, sender and subject line (thematic thread). Direct quoting in this way enables any receiver of a posting to check whether the reference to a previous contribution is correct (thereby ensuring that the current author is not commenting on a distorted representation of the point of view of his/her opponent). It also enables a reader to trace back a discussion to its origins and thus enable receivers who did not follow a certain discussion from the beginning to join in at a later date. The use of direct quoting is a sign for the awareness of discussants that they are not only communicating with the author(s) of the message(s) they refer to, but that there is a group of anonymous, silent 'listeners' who might also be interested in the topic under consideration but who might not have followed the discussion from the beginning. This kind of reference between follow-up postings was most frequently used by discussants of the LINGUIST list, but rarely in the ETHNO list where different forms of reference were used (see below).

The following extract 2 shows an example of a typical reactive posting in the ETHNO list.

## Extract 2:

'CE1 [first name] asks how can we proceed if we reject probabilistic decision theory on the grounds that it is inadequate or incoherent.
However, the task is not to respecify the enterprise of subjective probability or figure out some alternative framework ahead of time. ...' (IE1, 8. Aug, ETHNO-List, disc. 1)

In the first sentence of this posting the author refers back to a previous message which he comments on in the remainder of his contribution. If we compare the kinds of reference in extracts 1 and 2 we find marked differences. In extract 2 the author obviously does not use the built-in software function for replying but rather paraphrases the previous contribution. Additionally, he mentions only the first name of the author of the previous message without quoting any further information.

Indirect quotation was frequently used by contributors of the ETHNO list. In the context of email discussions the use of indirect quotation poses a problem for those readers who have not followed a discussion from the beginning or who have missed (or skipped) some contributions, because it provides only minimal cues to identify the contribution which the current posting refers to.

Additionally, in ETHNO discussions thematic threads are not consistently used to mark discussion topics during the whole time they are conducted. Instead discussants use thematic threads in a playful manner to allude to current political or social events or to yield ironic effects which are caused by the relation between thematic thread and content of a message. Therefore, the ways of establishing thematic connections between messages (and thus the way coherence is created in a discussion) in the ETHNO list reveals that contributors are not concerned with 'outsiders' who might join in a discussion at any time, but that they produce their messages mainly for an in-group of discussants who have followed a topic from the beginning.

## 4.5  Conclusion

The quantitative results seemed to suggest that scholarly email discussions form a single genre which can be characterised by features of academic letter writing as well as oral communication, thus showing the typical 'hybrid' text-characteristics which are attributed to email communication in many investigations. This first view would lead to the conclusion that a stable genre which we could call 'scholarly email discussion list posting' has already evolved. However, a closer qualitative analysis of one single textual feature, namely quoting, revealed that there are marked differences between postings to the two lists. Direct quoting was typical for reactive postings to the LINGUIST list, whereas indirect quoting was typical for contributions to the ETHNO list.

Thus, the question posed at the beginning of this chapter cannot be answered unambiguously - it is impossible to speak of a single genre of 'scholarly email postings', rather it seems that different sub-genres have evolved which share certain linguistic features on the macro level, but also reflect the orientation of contributors towards discussions and the discussion process in their micro-textual structure. Therefore it seems sensible to differentiate between a 'genre' of asynchronous email communication which comprises different 'sub-genres', a differentiation which Swales' conception does not allow for, but which is provided by Mauranen's (1993) functional and Berkenkotter and Huckin's (1995) sociocognitive approaches. The results of this study suggest that subscribers to the two different discussion lists seem (apart from their overall aim of discussing certain interesting and relevant topics) to be oriented towards slightly different communicative goals: whereas LINGUIST contributors produce their texts also for an overhearing audience, ETHNO subscribers seem to adopt an 'insider' perspective which may exclude others from the discussions. A plausible explanation might be that people mailing to the LINGUIST list, with its high volume of messages and large and varied readership, realise that they cannot assume acquaintance in their readers with previous postings, while contributors to the ETHNO list, with its tighter focus and possibly more assiduous user group, can safely take knowledge of this context in their readers for granted.

## Notes

(1)  I restrict the use of the term 'discussion list' to academic discussion lists in the context of this paper (although there are estimations that up to 40,000 public discussion lists exist on the Internet; McElhearn, 1996, personal email). They should be distinguished from newsgroups which cover a wide range of popular, social and scientific topics and which can be joined by anybody who has access to the Internet. Scholarly discussion lists, on the other hand, can only be joined if a user sends a 'subscribe' command to the respective server's Internet address. Thus, discussion list subscribers are, in principle, those persons who are in some sense members of the discourse community (Swales, 1990) of a certain academic field and not netsurfers who found a discussion list by chance.

(2)  This view presupposes a continuum between a 'spoken' and 'written' pole. For the moment I shall let this assumption go unquestioned.

# 5. The use of communicative resources in internet video conferencing

Pirkko Raudaskoski

## 5.1 Introduction

Desktop video conferencing is becoming increasingly available in both institutional and private settings as a cheaper alternative to traditional video conferencing (Ehlers and Steinfiel, 1992). This chapter reports on a study of human-human interactions mediated through desktop video conferencing and explores the ways in which communicative resources different from those used in face-to-face communication are used in the ongoing activity. The study focuses particularly on how the video pictures sent and received are oriented to and employed as communicative resources.

The cornerstone of the 'information society', the Internet, has brought text-based communication towards synchronous interaction. For example, the Talk program in Unix allows two users to share the screen for simultaneous typing and the text version of Internet Relay Chat can connect a number of discussants at the same time. [Editors' note: Todd and Walker discuss the use of such facilities in Chapter 7]. But recently desktop video conferencing systems have become available for use over modem lines and the Internet. These systems can provide a moving image of a participant, so that the 'other' is represented visually (as themselves, not as a 'blockie', 'avatar' or other such representation of a person in the visual multi-user domains, for example Bowers *et al*. 1996). In CU-SeeMe video conferencing, it is possible to link two sites via video picture, sound and text (typed either on the video picture itself or in a separate Talk/Chat window). According to some experts, CU-SeeMe, the video conference program which was used to link two student groups in a set of seminars analysed below, 'may be the harbinger of things to come' (Angiolillo *et al.*, 1997, p. 64).

My data come from a university course (from Spring 1995) in which a 'personal' (as opposed to institutionalised video studio) video conferencing program on the Internet was used. This low-cost, though highly effective, video conferencing solution resembles those applied in other educational contexts, as reported in Sattler (1995). The data recorded from this 'virtual seminar' makes it possible not only to see how the seminar was managed via the link, but also to find out what was new and different from face-to-face and audio interactions (or even from video studio and TV-watching activities). From general observations and a closer data analysis, the conclusion can be drawn that, depending on the material setting of the room and the position of computers / camera / loudspeakers, there will emerge different zones of interaction not only in the on-screen space but also within a 'real' room.

One aspect of interaction that to my knowledge has not been researched is typing activity on the video screen itself. This can go on even when the audio connection is working. In the search for 'life-like' video conferencing systems (Gaver *et al.*, 1992; Buxton, 1997), typing on one's own video picture, which emphasises the picture as a mediated representation of the other space, has not been of interest to researchers. Indeed, typing on one's picture has been considered a 'primitive' form of communication (Sattler, 1995, p. 112) in comparison to the use of a separate text entry window on the one hand and an audio link on the other. However, when used in addition to the mediated video and audio, plus the Chat window, the use of semi-permanent scrolling text on the video picture gives another dimension to the interpretation of what is going on. Text-on-video has some interesting characteristics. When the participants take advantage of the opportunity to type on the transmitted image of themselves rather than using the Chat window, the receivers do not have to find the correct video frame to match the speaker. The text on the picture therefore has a property in common with the person's voice - the receiver is able easily to locate the source of the words. However, unlike natural voice sounds, the text does not disappear immediately - as more words are added, the text overflows from the single scrolling line on the video frame. Often the last part of the text is left on the screen, becoming a disembodied piece of language as the participants move forward to the next activity in the situation.

## 5.2   Methodology - the interactionist approach

Many studies on human-computer interaction deal with sharing, be it sharing the linguistic code as a tool to act with the computer, or, particularly in the case of virtual reality and video conferencing, the feeling of shared presence. Often research on these topics is conducted by asking the users afterwards how they felt about the encounter (Muhlbach *et al.*, 1995). The methodology used in this study is to analyse these semiotically complex encounters using Conversation Analysis, in order to grasp the interpretative work and participation frameworks (Goodwin, 1986, p. 285) observable in the situation. The approach is that of interaction studies, which is an umbrella term for analyses in which different human interactional environments are studied to better understand how the individual realises the communicative potential in their use of language, gaze direction, posture and gestures. In this view, language is strongly rooted in the situation, and its meaning cannot be divorced from the moment of its use. Thus, meaning making is studied as a local and emerging phenomenon in ongoing human practices in real time. In the words of Boden (1990, p. 200), 'structure is actualized in the interactional work of temporally and spatially located activities whose constitutive meaning is discovered in the lived-work of producing them.'

## 5.3 The data

### Context

Data was gathered on CU-SeeMe video conferencing from a one month teaching experiment undertaken in a university in Finland (McIlvenny, 1995). The Internet was used to give a course in two places at the same time; one group of students were Finns in Finland, the other group were Swedes in Sweden, and English was used as lingua franca. The teacher and the students used Internet facilities to exchange ideas and papers. As part of the course, video conference sessions were held once a week to give the students an opportunity to give presentations, to provide direct, 'face-to-face' feedback, and in general to talk to each other and to see each other in a seminar-type situation. CU-SeeMe and also Maven, an audio conference program used in some sessions, were freeware from the Internet. They enabled on-line meetings between the two student groups who otherwise would not and could not have 'met' each other 'face-to-face', at least not in the framework of the university seminar in question. Thus, the setting of the conferencing was 'unorthodox' in the sense that desktop video conferencing was used to link two student groups (from 6 to 12 in number at each end), using several monitors to convey the black and white video pictures to facilitate the interaction between the two sites.

### The recordings

At the Finnish end the site was in fact an office-turned-into-a seminar/video conference room and at the Swedish end, a computer lab. Figure 1 shows the general outline of the room used for the video conferences in Finland, while Figure 2 is a snapshot of screen activity in the middle of a seminar, taken from the recording camera No. 5.

During the seminars, in addition to the two recordings made in the room in Finland (Figure 1), a third recording was collected from another site connected to a so-called

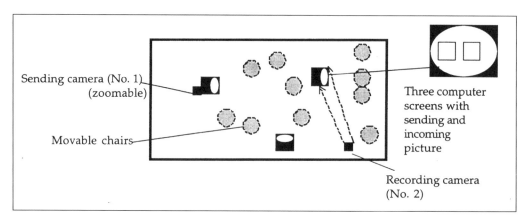

*Figure 1. Outline of the room configuration in Finland.*

reflector. This third recording made it possible to see clearly what was written on the video pictures. This additional data was crucial if we were to be able to investigate the role of written interaction in the seminars. And as the Finnish end was video recorded with the sending camera and another camera in the corner of the room, all talk and typing sounds were available for the analysis. The third recording could be used to fill in the information of what was typed on the screen.

*Figure 2. A Finn discussing with Swedish students in a seminar session.*

## CU-SeeMe as MeSee(what)UC

One of the important differences between face-to-face discussions and those which take place through video conferencing is that, via the feedback screen which displays the camera image of the user, we can monitor what the other can see of ourselves, and vice versa. This is quite an extension to our normal face-to-face awareness of the self and the other (Schutz, 1980) . However, particularly in those video conference setups which involve a changing camera angle, information about the nature of one's own video picture is required because otherwise it is impossible to estimate how one is seen by the other.

## 5.4 Data analysis

The observations discussed below come from the first session, a broadcast with a fixed camera view (5.5 hours of data). In the second section, orientations to the incoming picture or the sending picture are described on the basis of the interaction when the camera view was zoomed in and out to give group shots or head shots of specific individuals (5 hours of data). The final section concentrates on how writing on the video screen was used as resource in the ongoing interaction.

### General observations

In their interaction, the participants usually constructed the situation as happening in two places (for example, 'this end', 'that end'). The Finnish students tended to objectify both the incoming and sent video picture, and also the sound from Sweden. Sometimes, communicating through video conferencing resulted in specific orientations of gaze and posture in the room; the participation framework of the Finnish students near the computer with a sending camera (No. 1 in Figure 1), loudspeakers, and video picture to type on gave clear indications that they felt themselves to be sharing a common space with their Swedish partners. To give an example, at one point, two female students at the Finnish end turned their heads away from the screen to look directly at the current speaker who was in the same room as they were, at exactly the same time. A closer examination showed that the head turns coincided with the moment when the camera showed a student in Sweden, situated in front of the camera, lifting her gaze from her papers towards the camera. This is a strong indication that the students treated the video picture of the Swedish student in the same way as if they were in a shared space with a non-active participant - we know that gazing at a non-active participant can cause discomfort to the target of the gaze (Heath *et al.* 1997, p. 328). A sensitive participant would therefore try to disguise the fact that they had been looking at such a target, perhaps by looking away as soon as the target risked becoming aware of their gaze.  Perhaps this was the explanation for the strange participation framework (for a participant in a video conference) of the two students.

### Orienting to the incoming and outgoing videopictures

Since the 'virtual' seminar took place in two geographically remote locations, the other of which was visible via a video picture, for the Finnish students who were speaking there were two options for orienting to those present in Sweden - either to look at the camera or to look at the video picture showing the Swedish students. In the first case, the current speaker would not be so much distracted from the other Finns, and the glances at the camera would be seen by participants at the Swedish site as glances at them - this would be the 'normal' way for a speaker to behave (i.e. not to look at the addressee all the time). However, the tendency was to 'talk to the screen', and thus forget about the fellow students in Finland. Only if an answer was negotiated by the whole group in Finland would the gaze of the current speaker shift from the screen to the camera. Therefore, the attention structure of an active participant in Finland was geared towards Sweden, unless their turn was negotiated in Finland.

Video conferencing can also influence turn design and lexical choices. A motionless video picture from one of the sites would act as an extra marker of turn allocation, especially when complemented by the use of 'over' to give the turn to the mediated 'others'. The video picture is an uncertain carrier of visual information to the other site - the speaker can be out of the picture or just moving into the picture. This uncertainty was reflected in the speakers' orientation to their video picture when they 'identified the current speaker' by formulating the turn beginning as 'this is X (here)'. Often the virtual visual depiction of the participants was accompanied by virtual sound - when the sound connection was slow, the turn of a Finnish speaker could be heard 'conversing' later at the Swedish end.

When they appeared on the screen of the two computers on the right in Figure 1, the video pictures of oneself on the screen were treated as metonyms, as icons of oneself. The computer with the incoming sound (to which the loudspeakers were connected), which was also near the camera, seemed to create a zone which affected the participation frameworks in the room. Proximity to this zone gave a feeling of being more a participant in the situation. In contrast, proximity to the other computers gave a feeling of being more of an observer.

### Typing on the video picture - the synchronous/asynchronous division in the making

When typing on the video screen is used as a way of communicating on-line, as in the present case study, there is a close-knit connection between the text and what is going on in the video picture: the written message is produced for a moment in the interaction and not as a general persistent message. However, typed talk on the video picture does not disappear unless the 'enter' or 'backspace' key is hit, or if the typist keys in a longer sentence, in which case it disappears slowly into the left border of the screen. In addition, unlike text-only synchronous computer conferencing programs, the visual information is also available for the receiver of the message. The time of writing can also be the time of reading, unlike in asynchronous written communication. Thus, typing on a video picture in on-line video conferencing differs considerably from, for example, e-mail messages which are received, edited and responded to asynchronously (cf. Bowers and Churcher, 1988, p. 129). Like Talk in Unix, editing on the video picture is done on-line, which is unlike the functioning of the Chat/Talk box in CU-SeeMe. This allows for the separate writing and sending of one's contribution so that the other only sees what one sends after it is completely composed. With the narrow, one-line space for the typing, text-on-image is necessarily linear, like speech, because there is no trace of the preceding discussion. Again, this is quite different from the Chat/Talk box, in which a trace of whole interaction is recoverable. Unlike the sound of the speaking voice which is available for the whole of the audience (even if they would not want to hear it), textual information, like signed languages, has to be seen to be integrated into the ongoing situation. Written texts are not usually immediately available for the onlookers, i.e. one has to concentrate on the computer screen if one wants to 'hear' what the others say. But sound can bypass even visual barriers.

Typing on the video picture during the seminars was a resource that, like seeing oneself in a video picture, the students had to learn to orient to and exploit. Though writing is considered rudimentary by comparison with the more sophisticated technologies of audio and video contact, the data provides intriguing material for researching the multimodal use of and borderline between spoken and written communication. Some examples are listed below:

## Typed text ignored
For instance, when the students came to the room in Finland, the Finnish video picture had the following question typed on it, 'where are the masks?' Nobody commented or otherwise oriented to the writing.

## Double check
Many times 'sound checking', or a confirmation of sound check, was done textually. For instance, a request from Finland about opening the microphone resulted in both spoken and typed answers 'oh but it's on' and 'it's on'.

## Additional information
In the very first video conference session, the students introduced themselves, giving their names and a short introduction to their interests and their research topic in the seminar. The teacher in Sweden and his helper in Finland typed the name on top of the video picture. Only the first names were given, and typing them was a feature of the

cross-cultural situation rather than signalling doubts about the audio line - Finns and Swedes do not necessarily know how the names from each country are spelled.

**Integral part of sequential interaction**
In this mode, typing on the screen is basically replacing speech. For instance, when a person's name (especially if she is not in the video picture) is typed on the screen by somebody at the other end of the link, this name on the screen can be interpreted as a summons. There were several variants of this usage:
*Typing as a first attempt*
> To get the attention of a person at the other end of the line via typing was often hard and the sound connection was relied on later on in the seminar.

*Multiple dialogues*
> Sometimes a separate dialogue from the ongoing audio connection emerged on the video picture. In Finland, the teacher's helper would type on the screen something that was meant to be read by the teacher in Sweden or by a person in the other site in Finland.

*'Normal' communication - transcribed text only*
> Long interactions without sound took place by typing on the video picture on a turn-by-turn basis.

*'Normal' speech and transcribed speech alternately*

Particularly in the first seminar in which the audio link was one-way, i.e. only one party could speak at a time, typing was used at the other end to 'talk'. For instance, at one point, the teacher's helper in Finland urges the teacher in Sweden to go on talking (there was doubt at the Swedish end whether they could be heard in Finland) by typing on the video picture: TALK NOW!!!!!!!!! PHIL. The teacher reacted to this, saying 'we are talking' though this could not be heard in Finland. The attempt at securing the intersubjective understanding of a working audio connection was not very successful, because of the choice of wording. TALK NOW was interpreted as 'why don't you start talking' instead of 'go on talking' as it was intended in the situation. As often happens with typing on the screen, the text was left there until further text was typed in. This had interactional consequences, as the 'moment of the turn' with its meaning passed, and the theoretical ambiguity (cf. Schegloff, 1984) of a disembodied written sentence could play a part in the unfolding interaction subsequently (see below). Later in the interaction, the teacher requested a typed confirmation about the status of reception at the other site. He formulated his words as a request for a special wording - 'Kerttu can you type that that's ok, you can hear us fine'. Kerttu's reply on the screen shows her orientation to the message as a request for typing certain words: WE CAN HEAR YOU FINE. This way, intersubjectivity about the meaning of the words on the screen is achieved and there is no danger of a 'wrong' reading at the Swedish end. Thus, increasing degrees of specificity are needed to resolve repair sequences and requests for clarification.

**Out of sequence**
Text on video picture can 'participate' for a longer period of time in the ongoing

interaction. To illustrate this, let us return to the previous example. Conversation analytical methodology can show how the 'perlocutionary effect' of a piece of text continues after its first locution.

The typed order (or appeal) TALK NOW!!!!!!!! PHIL was left on the video picture. Later, a student in Sweden reacted to this earlier contribution 'out of' sequence in the unfolding turn-taking from the 'sender's' point of view - she typed (making a spelling mistake) phil is takhing all the time. At the same time, the visual message conveys to Finland the orienting to and interpretation of the encouragement to speak. The student interpreted the turn on the screen as a next speaker selection.

The response and accompanying interpretation to Kerttu's earlier turn was done out of the context of its situated production. Indeed, the writing on the Finnish video picture at that point (TALK NOW!!!!!!!! PHIL) was not 'replacing Kerttu's voice', i.e. she did not utter it in that place in the interactional sequence. Therefore, even if the contribution from Sweden in no way disturbed what was going on interactionally, the connection between the production of Kerttu's contribution and the later response was abstracted away and artificial, though not for the Swedish party. In transient face-to-face turns-at-talk, the second pair part of an adjacency pair can come later, but the intervening talk must be a side sequence related to the first pair part. Any turn-at-talk can be addressed later in talk, but it cannot be understood as being about a previous turn-at-talk unless it is marked to be so (cf. Schegloff, 1988, 131). The process of meaning making is not mutual at this point, but the reader/user of the piece of text on the video picture interacts with the text rather than its author by choosing this next.

## 5.5 Conclusion

In CU-SeeMe video conferencing seminars, securing mutual understanding becomes a joint achievement. The video-mediated images of the 'other' and of oneself objectify the interactional situation, and they may result in observation rather than participation, displacing the participant from direct to indirect social experience. The material circumstances make it such that typing on the video picture, because of its non-transient character, is similar to disembodied writing. A participant's motivated 'transcription of speech' can therefore become part of abstract asynchronous communication in which the production and interpretation of text are separated: we get a glimpse of the synchronous/asynchronous division in the making. In this case study, we can see a transition from mediated human-human interaction towards mediated human-text interaction.

## Acknowledgements

This contribution was written during a visit to the Communication Department of Aalborg University, Denmark, made possible by a research scholarship from the Academy of Finland. I would like to thank Paul McIlvenny for his useful comments.

# 6. The pragmatics of orality in English, Japanese and Korean computer-mediated communication

Robert J. Fouser

Narahiko Inoue

Chungmin Lee

## 6.1 Introduction

For many people in non-English speaking countries, the Internet could easily be called the 'Englishnet' because of the dominance of the English language. The Internet, however, is only one of many methods for exchanging computer-mediated messages. In Japan and Korea, people exchange computer-mediated messages in their native languages through public and commercial online systems. Unlike the Internet, which does not provide universal access to non-Roman character sets, these systems are fully capable of transmitting messages in the Japanese and Korean languages within each nation. Little of this computer-mediated communication activity makes its way onto the Internet because few computer systems outside Japan and Korea have the character sets for writing these languages.

In recent years, computer-mediated communication has become increasingly popular in Japan and Korea. In the public sphere, chatrooms and newsgroups, similar to those found on the Internet and on commercial online services found in the West, have emerged as the most popular forums. Like their counterparts elsewhere, users of chatrooms and newsgroups in Japan and Korea have altered accepted practices in writing and have added new orthographic devices, such as smileys, to their writing. These devices represent attempts to convey orality — the dialogic spontaneity of spoken and non-verbal language — in online messages, which remain in a written mode (Wignall, 1993). Wignall's definition of orality is based on the work of Walter Ong (1982), who developed a series of measures to compare orality with literacy in his seminal work *Orality and Literacy: The Technologizing of the Word*. Central to Ong's discussion of orality is the effect of context and memory on communication. In oral cultures, knowledge has to be memorised and all communication is oral, usually involving a community of speakers and listeners. To preserve knowledge and communicate it effectively, oral cultures rely on mnemonic narratives that include proverbs, rhyming, and dramatisation (for a complete discussion, see Chapter 3 of Ong, 1982).

Despite the development of a large repertoire of orthographic devices to show orality in Korean and Japanese, these devices are constrained by the orthographic system and keyboard inputting techniques in both languages. The desire to convey orality in online communication may be 'universal', but the methods for doing so remain constrained by the orthographic system and technical capabilities of word-processing. An important research question, then, is how do the orthographic system and technical capabilities of word processing constrain the representation of orality in online communication across languages?

Orality, however, is not only constrained by orthography and technology, it is also constrained pragmatically. In spoken language, the use of gestures, voice modulation and other extralinguistic devices is not equally distributed across speech acts. Likewise, the conveyance of orality in online communication through orthographic deviations differs according to speech act. It also differs according to language, which leads to another important research question - how does orality vary according to speech act and across languages? Answering these questions will help us gain a greater understanding of what is universal and what is language- and culture-specific about computer-mediated communication.

To answer the above questions, we have chosen to compare the occurrence of orality in public messages — chatrooms and newsgroups — in English, Japanese, and Korean. Comparing phenomena in Japanese and Korean with those in English is useful because the amount of research and the number of users in English is greater than in those of Japanese or Korean. These three languages make for an interesting comparison because each language has a different type of writing system and because spoken and written pragmatic and rhetorical traditions differ in each language.

## 6.2 Background information - writing systems and word-processing

Before discussing the study, we will discuss the relevant terminology, the writing systems of the three languages, and word-processing techniques in the three languages.

For this study, we have followed the terminology used by Sampson (1985) and Coulmas (1989). By 'writing system', we mean the overall structure and organisation of graphically represented units of language. We use 'graph' to refer to the visible marks in a writing system, and 'orthography' to refer to the standards and conventions of organising graphs within a system. A 'script' is a set of graphs that are used together; a script is a collection of graphs and not a language. The Roman script contains 26 graphs, known commonly as letters. Roman script is used for many writing systems around the globe, such as English, French, Turkish, or Vietnamese. Some writing systems, such as Japanese, are composed of more than one script.

Another set of important definitions refers to the type of graphs used in a writing system. Sampson (1985) drew a useful distinction between semasiographic systems of writing, which represent concepts independently of the structures of language through icons, and glottographic systems of writing, which represent the structures of the language graphically. Though Unger and DeFrancis (1995) argue that a semasiographic system is technically impossible because all writing must reflect the spoken language, I interpret Sampson's discussion as referring to the theoretical possibility of a system of writing independent of spoken language. Sampson (1985) further divided glottographic systems into logographic systems in which graphs represent the morphemes and lexical elements in the language, and phonographic systems in which graphs represent the phonetic features of the language. Semasiographic systems of writing are rare, but a commonly found example would be symbols in airports or on highways and emoticons, such as :-). The major division in writing systems in the world is between logographic and phonographic. Phonographic systems include those in which graphs represent syllables, segments of sound, and phonetic features of articulation. Table 1 illustrates Sampson's scheme for describing writing systems.

We will begin our discussion of the writing system of each language with English. Although the English writing system is based on a phonographic use of the Roman script, the historical development of English has given it a strong logographic element. Words that entered the language after the Norman Conquest in 1066, for example, are in many cases spelled with little relationship to the sound of their present-day pronunciation, meaning that they are analysed by readers according to the organisation of the graphs, and not the sounds that the graphs represent. In recent years, there has been a marked increase in the use of acronyms, which become logographic representations of a long string of words. The Internet has stimulated the production of a wide variety of logographs, such as IMHO, LOL, BTW, and FYI, in addition to the ubiquitous @ sign. Logographic elements in English give the language greater visual variety, which makes it easier for readers to follow lines of text (Sampson, 1985). The logographic distinction among 'to', 'too', and 'two' is one such example.

Japanese writing is a combination of the phonographic syllabary, *kana*, and logographs borrowed from Chinese, or *kanji*. The *kana* is composed of two scripts,

| | | |
|---|---|---|
| *Semasiographic:* | ♨ ☄ ⚐ ▷ | (common icons) |
| *Logographic:* | 我住在倫敦. | (Chinese) |
| | I /*_\ @ [(*)] | ("ASCIIese") |
| *Phonographic* | | |
|   Syllabic: | 私はロンドンに住んでいます. | (Japanese) |
|   Segmental: | I live in London. | (English) |
| | Vivo en Londres. | (Spanish) |
| | ai liv in landən. | (IPA/English) |
|   Featural: | 저는 런던에 살고 있습니다. | (Korean) |

*Table 1. Comparison of different writing systems.*

*hiragana*, which is used for extensively for morphemes, and *katakana*, which is used for words of foreign (though not Chinese) origin. *Kana* evolved from Chinese graphs in the 8th and 9th centuries. Japanese is the only language in the world composed of three different scripts, each with a different role in the writing system. Like English, Japanese can be difficult to write, which caused some Japanese people to advocate a switch to Roman script in the early years of the 20th century. For the reader, however, the use of *kanji* (Chinese logographs) makes reading easier because it greatly increases the visual distinctiveness of the writing system. A purely phonographic system for Japanese would slow reading considerably because the Japanese language has relatively few sounds, and hence, and a large number of homophones. The necessity for visual distinction among the large number of homophones in Japanese explains why efforts to eliminate *kanji* or reduce their number have largely failed (Sampson, 1985; Coulmas, 1989; see Twine, 1991 for a detailed discussion grammatical and orthographic modernisation of the Japanese language in the late 19th century). Although, as Unger and DeFancis (1995) pointed out, early Chinese logographs contain a phonological element in which parts of the character indicate the pronunciation, most characters contain a distinct lexical or morphological meaning, which conforms to Sampson's (1985) definition of a logograph. In addition, the distinct shape of each graph matches the Sampson definition.

The Korean system, in contrast to English and Japanese, is a masterpiece of linguistic engineering. The Korean script, *hangul*, is a phonographic script in which some of the 24 (originally 28) graphs depict the points of articulation of all of the phonemes in the Korean language. These graphs are then combined together into units that correspond with syllable boundaries in Korean. Diphthongs are also made by combining the graphs for pure vowels together. *Hangul* was invented in 1443 (promulgated in 1446) specifically for the Korean language independently of existing scripts in the world at the time. Before the invention of *hangul*, the Korean writing system used Chinese logographs exclusively. *Hangul* became the dominant form of writing only in the 20th century, and *hanja* (Chinese logographs) continue to be used in South Korea, mainly in academic writing and newspaper headlines, but have been eliminated from official orthography in North Korea (Sampson, 1985; Kim 1990). *Hangul* orthography, however, has been the subject of much controversy because the Korean language includes a number of morphophonemic constraints that cause one *hangul* graph to be pronounced differently according to the phonological environment. The current *hangul* orthography, which was standardised in 1933, is based on morphological boundaries, many of which originate in the pronunciation of Chinese logographs. This means that many words are written differently from how they are pronounced. The rules that govern phonological changes in Korean are regular, but, as with English spelling, they need to be memorised. Until the 20th century, *hangul* orthography followed surface phonological rules rather than the deeper morphological structure (Sampson, 1985; Lee, 1963).

## 6.3 Method

### *Hypothesis*

To answer the research questions set out above, we developed the following informal hypothesis:

> Online users in these three languages use a variety of semasiographs, logographs, and orthographic deviations to convey orality, but the extent of these additions and deviations varies among the three languages according to type of writing system and prevailing cultural traditions regarding the burden of contextuality.

Based on this hypothesis, we derived the following sub-hypotheses on each of the languages under discussion. With English, we expected to find a modest number of additions and deviations because the English writing system combines phonographic and logographic elements, making it more susceptible to alteration than Japanese. As the most commonly used language on the Internet and in computer-mediated communication, English is subject to the largest number of idiosyncratic additions and deviations from the largest number of users. Alteration in English is constrained, however, by logographic elements that make serious deviations difficult to understand and by a writing tradition that places the burden of contextuality on writers to express themselves clearly.

With Japanese, we expected the smallest number of additions and deviations because Japanese writing is based on a mixed system of writing that combines the *kana* syllabary with Chinese characters, which are logographic. In both types of writing, orthographic alteration distorts the graphs, which destroys readability. Although Japanese writing traditions place the burden of contextuality on the reader, which encourages writers to express themselves honestly in an aesthetically pleasing style, the writing system constrains the number of additions and deviations that are possible without distorting meaning excessively.

With Korean, we expected to find the greatest number of additions and deviations because the Korean writing system is a featural system that closely reflects the morphophonemic structure of the language through a small number of phonetic graphs organised into a variety of easily distinguishable syllables. Korean follows a deep orthography that indicates only irregular phonological changes. In online communication, however, we predict that, to give their messages orality, writers will follow a shallow orthography that corresponds closely to spoken Korean. This will, along with various additions, result in considerable deviation from standard Korean orthography. Like Japanese, the Korean rhetorical tradition places the burden of contextuality on readers. Writers are expected to express themselves freely, which contributes to the expression of orality in online communication.

## Data collection

To test the above hypotheses, we gathered two types of data in all three languages - synchronous chatroom data and asynchronous public newsgroup postings.

   Chatroom and newsgroup data were collected because differences in writing systems and word-processing programs affect the speed at which users can input language into the system, which in turn affects the type and number of orthographic deviations and additions.  Collecting both types of data gives us a balanced view of different types of orality in all three languages. Inputting *hangul* graphs in a Korean word-processing program is similar to inputting Roman graphs on an English keyboard.  The process of inputting Japanese, however, is more complicated.  The most common method of inputting Japanese is the FEP (Front End Processor) which is a program that converts *kana* into *kanji* directly.  Because there are 49 *kana*, they have to be mapped onto the keyboard in combination with the shift key.  *Kana* can be inputted as either *hiragana* or *katakana* and toggled back and forth with a special key.  Another choice is to use Roman letters to input *kana*, which are mapped to specific combinations of Roman letters.  With *kanji*, however, there is no one-to-one mapping system because many *kanji* have a different pronunciation.  To give the writer a clear choice of which *kanji* to use, the program parses the sentence grammatically into words and phrases and presents a choice of common *kanji* compounds with the same pronunciation at the bottom of the screen.  The writer then looks at the compounds and chooses the appropriate one to input on the screen.  This process take considerably more time than inputting graphs in Korean and English. (The Korean system for inputting Chinese characters is similar to Japanese.  Chinese characters, however, are rarely used in computer-mediated communication in Korea.)

   Comparing orality in chatroom and newsgroup data is also important in determining the effect of the synchronous environment of the chatroom on orality.  Does 'real-time' increase orality, or does orality increase when users have more time to 'compose' orality in asynchronous newsgroup postings?  How do patterns of chatroom and newsgroup orality vary across the three languages?  How do the writing systems and word-processing systems influence orality in chatroom and newsgroup postings?

   The amount of data was roughly uniform across all three languages - about 800 lines of chatroom data, and 2,200 lines of Usenet newsgroup data.  More newsgroup data were collected to compensate for the length of newsgroup messages and longer opening and closing sequences in newsgroup messages.  To obtain a broader range of data, an attempt was also made to collect the data at various times of the day and on different days.  Table 2 illustrates the main sources of data for each language.

   In all cases, the researchers logged on to the chatroom, but did not participate actively in the chat for fear of influencing the direction of the chat.  This issue is significant in Japan and Korea where age and social status influences speech levels in any interaction.  Local telephone calls after the first three minutes are charged by the minute in Korea and Japan, but are not in the United States.  Local telephone charges are expensive in Japan, which forces many users to login after 11:00 p.m. when phone rates go down.

| | Online Chat (source/amount) | Newsgroup (source/amount) |
|---|---|---|
| *Korean* | HITEL (national commercial) | han.rec.humor han.misc.misc |
| | 800 lines | 2,000 lines |
| *Japanese* | NIFTY-Serve (national commercial) | fj.rec.comics fj.misc. |
| | 800 lines | 2,400 lines |
| *English* | Voyager.net (local commercial) | friends list alt.angst |
| | 800 lines | 2,200 lines |

*Table 2. Background information on data.*

### Data coding and analysis

As shown in Table 3, we developed a coding system to analyse data across the three languages quantitatively. We then conducted a qualitative analysis of data from each language after coding the data. The unit of analysis for the coding scheme was the utterance, which in most cases consisted of one turn in chatroom discourse, and sentences in newsgroup postings. The case of the coding systems was limited to five expressive speech acts (greetings, apologies, pleasure/happiness, sadness, praise/compliments) according to Searle's (1976) taxonomy. We chose to limit the coding to these basic expressives to see how the use of orality related to a defined set of speech acts that could be compared across the three languages. Expressives are common in online discourse and lend themselves well to the expression of orality, even in situations that are constrained by the writing system and word processing capabilities. We also wanted to analyse a relatively large amount of data to capture the diverse range of phenomena in the three languages, but time constraints prevented us from analysing every utterance in the data. The anonymity inherent in computer-mediated communication prevented us from gathering data on age and sex of the participants; instead, we attempted to deduce the age and sex of participants from the style and register of their language. To code deviations and additions, four categories were established - semasiographic, logographic, phonographic, and 'no orality' (those utterances with no sign of orality).

The data were analysed separately by the researcher who collected the data for his native language, Fouser for English, Inoue for Japanese, and Lee for Korean. The data were first classified according to speech act and then analysed according to the above categories. For the purposes of this study, standard orthography was classified as those practices of writing that are commonly considered standard in writing in the three languages. Those deviations and additions that showed attempts to lengthen words, add emphasis, or reproduce sandhi phenomena (i.e. modification of sound of word caused by context) were classified as phonographic deviations. In addition, orthographic deviations in which graphs were used to spell words phonetically in a

*Unit of Analysis:* Utterance

*Case:* Speech Act

*Topics:* Expressive Speech Acts

    Greetings

    Apologies

    Pleasure/Happiness

    Displeasure/Sadness

    Praise/Compliments

*Coding Categories:*

    Semasiographic

    Logographic

    Phonographic

    No Orality

*Table 3. Coding scheme for data analysis.*

pattern that deviated from standard orthography were classified as phonographic deviations. Logographic deviations included deviant patterns in the use of logographs and the addition of new symbols to represent morphemes or lexical items within the utterance. Semasiographic deviations included the addition of emoticons and other extralinguistic symbols. Some semasiographic deviations were expressed in Roman, *hangul, kana* or *kanji* script, but these were classified as semasiographic in cases where they were extraneous to the linguistic structure of the utterance. Table 4 gives examples of deviations and additions.

After the data were coded and analysed according to the above coding scheme, each researcher made language-specific qualitative observations on the data.

## Results and discussion

Results from coding of the data are described in Table 5 on and Table 6.

The results confirmed our hypothesis for English and Korean, but were equivocal for Japanese. For English, we found that logographic and semasiographic additions and deviations were more common that phonographic ones. For Korean, we found that phonographic deviations accounted for a large percentage of all orality phenomena.

In the case of Japanese, however, we found a greater use of semasiographic additions than predicted and a wider range of phonographic deviations and additions. Japanese word-processors have a function that automatically stores semasiographs, such as ^.^, in the system, which gives users easy access to such symbols, particularly

| | Semasiographic | Logographic | Phonographic |
|---|---|---|---|
| *Korean* | ＾ ＾ ♪ ♥ | ??? Mr CNN | ～ ㅎㅎ ㄷ 당 |
| *Japanese* | ^.^ ^^/ ^^; 笑 | ? ヨカッタ おk | ～～ --- バイバーイ |
| *English* | :) =) =P {{{x}}} | !! m/f lol IMHO | hiya cya duz hehe |

*Table 4. Examples of deviations and additions in data.*

59

| | Total | No Orality | Semasiographic | Logographic | Phonographic |
|---|---|---|---|---|---|
| *Korean* | | | | | |
| greeting | 110 | 35 (31%) | 10 (9.4%) | 15 (14%) | 50 (45.6%) |
| apology | 5 | 2 (40%) | 0 | 0 | 3 (60%) |
| pleasure | 85 | 4 (4.7%) | 0 | 3 (3.5%) | 78 (91.8%) |
| sadness | 36 | 5 (14.1%) | 0 | 5 (14.1%) | 26 (71.8%) |
| praise | 2 | 1 (50%) | 0 | 0 | 1 (50%) |
| *Japanese* | | | | | |
| greeting | 304 | 4 (1.3%) | 70 (23%) | 161 (53%) | 69 (22.7%) |
| apology | 8 | 2 (25%) | 3 (37.5%) | 2 (25%) | 1 (12.5%) |
| pleasure | 27 | 0 | 15 (55.6%) | 7 (25.9%) | 5 (18.5%) |
| sadness | 10 | 2 (20%) | 2 (20%) | 4 (40%) | 2 (20%) |
| praise | 36 | 1 (2.8%) | 5 (13.8%) | 15 (41.7%) | 15 (41.7%) |
| *English* | | | | | |
| greeting | 175 | 120 (68.5%) | 20 (11.5%) | 15 (8.5%) | 20 (11.5%) |
| apology | 25 | 4 (16%) | 5 (20%) | 15 (60%) | 1 (4%) |
| pleasure | 82 | 0 | 14 (17.6%) | 44 (52.9%) | 24 (29.5%) |
| sadness | 25 | 15 (60%) | 2 (8%) | 5 (20%) | 3 (12%) |
| praise | 3 | 2 (66.6%) | 0 | 1 (33.3%) | 0 |

*Table 5. Results from coding of online chat data.*

in the chatroom setting. The popularity of comic books (manga) in Japan may help explain the relatively large number of visually stimulating semasiographs and phonographic additions and deviations. The latter occur regularly in comics, and are to a certain degree regularised. The use of a small *katakana* /tsu/ to indicate a final glottal stop is an example of the influence of comics.

All three languages showed some similarity regarding speech acts with greetings being the most common speech act in chatroom situations across all three languages. Greetings appear frequently in chatrooms as participants enter and leave. An active chatroom will have many more greetings than a less active one. Beyond greetings, English and Korean had more in common, particularly in the use of speech acts to express pleasure and sadness. Apologies and praise were found relatively infrequently in English and Korean, which perhaps reflects a greater sense of informality in English

|  | Total | No Orality | Semasiographic | Logographic | Phonographic |
|---|---|---|---|---|---|
| *Korean* |  |  |  |  |  |
| greeting | 32 | 22 (68.7%) | 0 | 8 (25%) | 2 (6.3%) |
| apology | 8 | 8 (100%) | 0 | 0 | 0 |
| pleasure | 48 | 2 (4.2%) | 0 | 7 (14.5%) | 39 (81.3%) |
| sadness | 5 | 0 | 3 (60%) | 1 (20%) | 1 (20%) |
| praise | 1 | 1 (100%) | 0 | 0 | 0 |
| *Japanese* |  |  |  |  |  |
| greeting | 103 | 79 (76.9%) | 2 (1.8%) | 22 (21.3%) | 0 |
| apology | 38 | 28 (73.7%) | 4 (10.5%) | 5 (13.2%) | 1 (2.6%) |
| pleasure | 6 | 1 (16.7%) | 4 (66.6%) | 0 | 1 (16.7%) |
| sadness | 1 | 0 | 0 | 1 (100%) | 0 |
| praise | 12 | 7 (58.4%) | 3 (25%) | 1 (8.3) | 1 (8.3%) |
| *English* |  |  |  |  |  |
| greeting | 40 | 13 (32.5%) | 10 (25%) | 15 (37.5%) | 2 (5%) |
| apology | 0 | 0 | 0 | 0 | 0 |
| pleasure | 24 | 1 (4.3%) | 4 (16.6%) | 16 (66.6%) | 3 (12.5%) |
| sadness | 48 | 17 (35.4%) | 5 (10.4%) | 16 (33.3%) | 10 (20.9%) |
| praise | 1 | 1 (100%) | 0 | 0 | 0 |

*Table 6. Results from coding of newsgroup data.*

and Korean online discourse. This is supported by the greater amount of praise and apologies found in the Japanese data. This reflects the emphasis on social distance and appropriate use of formulaic expressions in speech between strangers in Japanese.

The data also revealed that young people, particularly teenagers, dominated chatrooms. The English data were the most diverse in age, whereas the Korean data reflected the predominance of teenagers in chatrooms. Newsgroup users in Japanese and Korean tended to be in their twenties, mostly university students, whereas English newsgroups show a wider range of age (when it is possible to tell).

Language-specific findings revealed several interesting phenomena. Many deviations and additions in English follow a regular pattern, forming part of an emerging 'online register'. Logographs such as IMHO, FYI, LOL, and semasiographic additions such as :-) have become common and are used routinely. Korean and Japanese show a more idiosyncratic pattern within broad regular patterns. English messages, particularly those in newsgroups, contain frequent references to spelling and correct grammar, where as remarks about usage did not appear in the Japanese and Korean data. This reflects the importance of grammatical and orthographic rules in the writer-centred English rhetorical tradition (Aronoff, 1994).

Korean users, on the other hand, prefer to create their own idiosyncratic phonetic spellings of commonly-used patterns. They also draw on dialects, foreign words, the language of TV comedians, and the language of traditional Korean oral tales known as *p'ansori* (Lee, 1994). Many phonetic deviations have become part of a growing CMC-based lexicon of phonetic spellings and emoticons that follows its own conventions while allowing for idiosyncratic variation (Park, 1997). Korean newsgroups reflect the formal and polite speech level found in letters with relatively few deviations and additions.

## 6.4 Conclusion

In this study, we found that orality in computer-mediated communication, particularly synchronous discourse, was constrained significantly by the writing system and word-processing technology. Despite these constraints, we found that users of online communications developed a variety of ways to convey orality in expressive speech acts by creating new expressions while drawing on slang, popular culture, and oral traditions. We also found that the 'standardisation of orality' has begun in English, which suggests that idiosyncratic orality may be fading from online communication in English as ever-growing number of users increases the demand for codification of conventions. It may also suggest that orality in online communication is rooted deeply in language-specific rhetorical traditions, which come to the fore as the number of users increases. Users of the three languages discussed here may be able to break away from the constraints of the writing system, but in doing so they come face to face with rhetorical traditions that impose demands for a new linguistic 'order'.

## – Part Two –
## New Media, New Behaviours

# 7. Multilingualism on the Net: language attitudes and use of talkers

Zazie Todd

Stephanie Walker

## 7.1. Introduction

Electronic talkers, or chat-sites, allow people from across the globe to 'talk' in real-time via their computer keyboards. This opens up tremendous possibilities. Much research has concentrated on the rôle-playing potentials of a communication medium in which no one can see who they are talking to, for example by pretending to be a different gender or different kind of person (Turkle, 1996). However, this chapter looks beyond the potentials within the systems themselves to the interactions between real-life and online variables. Specifically, it draws on social psychology to examine what happens when members of different speech communities communicate via online chat-sites ('talkers').

Chat-sites are virtual spaces usually organised using a geographical metaphor, in that different areas are seen as different rooms or places within the same area. This chapter investigates talkers (written in a code called NUTS) to which users connect using telnet. While the commands vary slightly from talker to talker, there are some general features which all NUTS-based talkers share. Anything that the users type directly is seen by other users as something that they have 'said'. A number of other commands give them the ability to emote actions (for example 'Jackie smiles'), to send messages in private to other users in the room, or to leave messages either on a general noticeboard or in users' private mail-boxes. Users are also encouraged to create their own profiles, giving information about themselves which other users can look at.

Virtual communication in this way is different in several ways from face-to-face communication. Ikeda (1994) has described three ways in which users compensate for the lack of ordinary background and non-verbal information. The profiles just mentioned fall under his category of 'name-card exchange', where users swap information rather like the exchange of  business cards.  This means that although they can't see the other person directly, they can read some information about them which is provided by that user.  A second way of compensating is 'ideographisation' which is found for example in the use of *smilies*  such as :-)  to represent concepts visually (see also Reid (1995)).  Finally there is also the 'verbalian' category which involves making things which would normally be non-verbal into verbal forms, as with the 'emote' command referred to above: for example, a user called Jackie might write 'Jackie hugs you'.  While other users can't see that you are smiling or looking friendly, you can type in the information in order to make it known.

There is a clear potential for the Internet to be used in second language acquisition. Gardner (1985) has shown that learners who seek out language-learning environments, such as television, videos, and contact with native speakers, do better than those who don't.  The Internet could clearly provide another language-learning environment, allowing a language learner to interact in real-time with native speakers, even when they are geographically far apart.   The Internet provides several different forms of language-learning environments.  Cononelos and Oliva (1993) studied the use of USENET news and email in an Italian language and culture class, and Trenchs (1996) studied the effects of beginners in the Spanish language generating email.  However, these studies were only concerned with the use of a static medium in which the language learner could practice the language without any direct real-time contact. Chat-sites provide a different environment in which the pace of communication is closer to that of face-to-face communication, and allows regular and frequent contact with native language speakers.  There are drawbacks of course, in particular the fact that type-based chat-sites do not involve pronunciation of words, the style of language used is likely to be relatively informal, and some aspects may be specific to electronic communication (Ikeda 1994).  In addition, the nature of the medium is that it is littered with typos.  Nevertheless it may allow for some kinds of useful, informal language practice.

Learning a second language successfully involves not just learning the language but also acquiring patterns of action appropriate to that culture (Gardner, 1985).  Electronic communication could therefore also be used to learn more about the culture of the other language group.  Another possible benefit is in terms of intergroup communication, since intergroup factors (such as perceived permeability of boundaries between language groups) also play a role (Garrett, Giles and Coupland 1989).   Electronic communication may be useful in circumstances where there is little or no opportunity for real-life contact with native speakers.  Meyrowitz (1997) has considered the ways in which different media (including electronic media) affect the boundaries between in- and out-group.  It is possible that if use of electronic communication can alter our perceptions of the boundaries between groups (including groups with which we have no 'real-life' contact), this could be beneficial to the second language learner.

## 7.2  Multilingualism and multinationalism on talkers

The study began by considering the extent to which multilingualism is naturally-occurring on chat-sites.  The log files of ten talkers were studied for periods of time

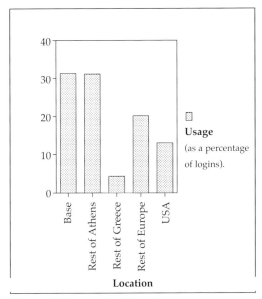

40

30

20

10

0

Usage

(as a percentage of logins).

Base | Rest of Athens | Rest of Greece | Rest of Europe | USA

**Location**

*Figure 1. Homecoming (Greece).*

varying between one to six weeks (since different operators have different practises, the time period was determined largely by what information was available). The log files record the time, source and username for every single login and logoff from the chat-site, along with other information about the running of the site. The data showed that most talkers were relatively insular in their make-up, with users generally coming from a relatively small geographical area. Our subsequent conversations with the talker operators confirmed that this meant the talkers were largely monolingual. For example, one talker studied was an Estonian-language chat-site, and although native Russians make up a small proportion of the Estonian population, Russian

language use on the chat-site was frowned upon and often led to adverse reactions from other people. The data for Homecoming (See Figure 1), a Greek talker based in Athens, is fairly typical. It can be seen that just over 30 per cent of the logins during the period of study came from the particular Internet site at which the talker is based, with an equal number coming from elsewhere in Athens. Although there are logins from the rest of Europe and the USA, the talker operator said that virtually all of these were either from Greeks abroad, using the system to keep in touch with friends, or from others with connections to Greece (e.g. second generation Greeks living in the USA).

Login data from one of the British talkers surveyed is shown in Figure 2. It can be seen from this that there is a wide range of nationalities using the talker - during the six week period, logins were recorded from 27 different countries. While the most common site for logins is Britain, the presence of so many different nationalities seemed significant. In fact during the time spent on the talker, it became apparent that although English was still the dominant language, many other languages were also in regular use (including Welsh, Dutch, French, German and Estonian). While we are not suggesting that this is necessarily unusual for an electronic talker, it did seem that this was the most multilingual of the talkers surveyed, and therefore it was chosen for a questionnaire study.

There are some problems with login data of this sort, in that it reflects only the numbers of logins from different sites, but not the amount of time spent on the talker. In addition it does not separate number of users from number of logins; this data could be collected only in terms of regular users as there is no way of determining who people logging in as 'guest' are, and on some occasions guests turn out to be regular

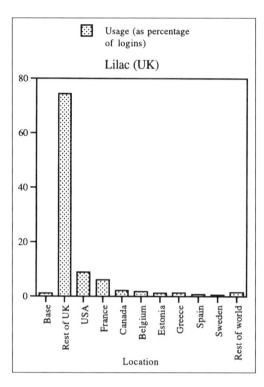

Figure 2.

users logging in as guests (for exmaple to avoid talking to a certain user, to play games, or because they have been banned under their usual alias). The length of logins is not measured from this data either and it was noted informally that some users spent considerably more time on the talker than others. Nevertheless the data gives a good general picture of the users of a talker over a period of time and the other ways of measuring all have biases of their own.

## 7.3 The questionnaire study

A short questionnaire using a seven-point Likert scale was designed to investigate users' views about language use on Lilac. Participants were recruited by a message left on the system's noticeboard, asking for volunteers, and questionnaires were sent out by email. On return, the headers were anonymised to ensure confidentiality for the participants. Altogether 11 British users and 14 users from elsewhere in Europe participated in this part of the study. Although this represents a small number of the total users of Lilac, all were high-usage registered users and so the sample is likely to be representative of regular Lilac users.

Participants were asked why they visited Lilac. Of the British users, all stated that they used Lilac to talk to other British people, but talking to people from abroad was rated almost equally as a reason for using the talker. The foreign users all said they used Lilac to talk to British people, but 65 per cent said that they also visited Lilac to talk to people from their own country. Thus it appears that on Lilac most users were talking to other nationalities, as well as their own.

The questionnaire distributed to foreign users contained some additional questions about their reasons for learning English. Traditionally social psychologists (Gardner 1985) have divided people into integrative learners (whose main reasons are to do with wanting social contact with the other language group) and instrumental learners (whose main reasons are more to do with such things as improving job prospects). However there is a recognition that both kinds of reasons can be important for some people. This was certainly found to be the case with participants in this study. Although integrative reasons (mean = 5.3) were rated slightly higher than instrumental ones (mean = 4.7), the different is very small and not statistically significant. All the users reported both kinds of reasons for learning English. They also showed a tendency to disagree with the statement 'I never feel quite sure of myself when speaking English online' (mean = 3.3). Only one of the foreign users surveyed said that he never spoke English on Lilac, although only three said that they spoke English most of the time.

There appeared to be a public/private distinction when it came to non-British users speaking in their own language. This was rated as always fine in private, but most non-British users reported that there had sometimes been occasions when it was found to cause problems with other users (not necessarily British) in public rooms. The foreign users all reported that time spent on Lilac (and on talkers in general) improved their use of English. This is exemplified by a comment added by one user who said 'Yes! Definitely. I wasn't speaking English at all before I started logging onto talkers regularly, but now that I've talked for about a year on Internet, my English has greatly improved.' This makes sense in terms of language practice, but as these are self-reports from language learners, further research is needed to carry out independent assessment to measure the extent of improvement that Internet use can lead to.

## 7.4 The French room and the language wars

An ethnographic study was also carried out during a period of transition which was caused by the creation of a French-language room for the French users. This was in response to an increasing number of French users on the talker. The talker operators asked one of the most frequent French users to write a description of the room in French, and this can be seen in Figure 3. The room description is what users saw on entering the room.

The immediate effect of the French room was an increase in the number of French users, who mostly occupied the area devoted to them rather than the general areas. In fact the room seemed very popular and led to an increase in both the amount of time that existing French users spent on the talker and in the number of registered users who were French. However, there were also some problems with non-French users, who didn't like the accompanying increase in the use of French in the general area. In these 'language wars', users started to complain about the use of French (and other languages) in the 'computer'. Some of the wizards (i.e. people who assisted in the running of the talker) even tried to ban French except in the French room. For these users, the room was not so much a means of welcoming French users and encouraging them to feel at home, but rather a separatist measure to keep them out of the general areas. Some users even went so far as to quit if people were speaking French in the general area.

The 'language wars' were gradually resolved by the talker operators. They established a rule that wizards couldn't move or discipline people for speaking French in the public rooms. They did allow wizards to encourage French users to move to their own room if they were logged on in any number. They also spent time explaining to users that all languages were welcome on the talker, and made a point of always discussing the matter with any users who publicly criticised people for speaking in languages other than English. This very hands-on policy seemed to improve tolerance for other languages on the chat-site.

```
"Vous voici dans le language...
Le language est un petit coin reserve aux frenchies ou a
ceux qui sont ouvert d'esprits. Au fond a droite un frigo
plein de friandises de toutes sortes vous attend.
Et si vous etes seul...laissez quelques mots sur le mur..."

(The language is a little corner reserved for the French
and those who are open-minded.  At the back on the right a
fridge full of delicacies awaits you.  And if you are
alone...leave a few words on the wall)
```

*Figure 3. Description of the French language room.*

## 7.5 Discussion and Conclusions

A number of lessons can be drawn from this study about the potential of Internet talkers for language-learning support. It is certainly the case that they allow for the possibility of second language learners having regular and frequent contact with native speakers. Despite the fact that this contact is only text-based (and therefore skills such as pronunciation cannot be practiced), all the learners of English as a second language who were surveyed reported that time spent using English on the talker improved their English in general. There was also a carry-over effect from this - it wasn't just the time spent using English on the talker which was felt to help improve English, but the fact that this also led to an increase in the amount of time spent using English or thinking in English in everyday life.

However, one point to came out of this study is that the way in which the talker was run seemed to be more important than the programming itself in fostering intercultural communication. Although the talker was reached via the Internet and could therefore be anywhere in the world, the country in which it was actually based appeared to be important to most users. It appears that the country, rather than the language in which the commands were written, was the influencing factor, as non-English-language talkers often still have English commands to make them easier to use for non-native (and not necessarily English) users. The creation of particular language rooms on their own, although very popular with the language group concerned, seemed to cause some other users to see it as a separatist measure and therefore to object to that language being used in general areas.

To summarise, this study has looked at a naturally-occurring case of multi-language use on Internet talkers. One problem is that although improvements in language ability were reported by the English-as-a-second-language group, these are only reported differences and no actual measures were taken. It is possible that users mainly showed increased confidence instead, although social psychological studies of language anxiety (Gardner, 1985) have shown that confidence is an important part of the language learning equation. We suggest that experimental work is needed in order to further study the possibilities for informal language practice on the net.

# 8. Maintaining the Virtual Community: use of politeness strategies in an email discussion group

Sandra Harrison

## 8.1 Introduction

Computer-mediated communication (CMC) has acquired a general reputation for lack of politeness, and in particular flaming - sending rude or aggressive emails - has attracted considerable research interest since the early work into the effects of its lack of social cues in CMC contexts (Kiesler, Siegel and McGuire, 1984). Yet computer-mediated communication has also generated considerable enthusiasm among participants, and for many it has been an important source of support and friendship (Rheingold, 1992). The popularity of email discussion lists is demonstrated by the number available which is estimated to be about 11,000 (Vitale, 1996). Although the overt purpose of these lists is often transactional, in practice a major part of their function is interactional - Korenman and Wyatt (1996) investigating 'group dynamics' in an email discussion list found that many respondents mentioned the 'sense of community' which they gained from participation (1996, p. 233) [See also Matthews, Chapter 9 of this volume].

The research discussed in this paper uses Brown and Levinson's (1987) work on politeness to investigate politeness strategies in the text of an exemplary email discussion. It examines a successful email discussion in order to establish some of the strategies which contributed to its success, and to perhaps provide a benchmark which could be used for comparison with less successful discussions. In this context, I have taken 'success' to mean that in general participants were satisfied with the themes chosen for discussion, that questions usually elicited a response and that participants could handle disagreement without hostility.

## 8.2 Politeness strategies

Central to Brown and Levinson's analysis of politeness strategies is the concept of 'face' and the 'face-threatening act' (1987, p.62). Face is one's 'public self-image', and Brown and Levinson distinguish between 'positive face', which is a person's desire to be liked, valued and understood; and 'negative face', which is a person's desire to act freely and without hindrance. Face can be threatened in many ways, for example a hearer's face may be threatened when a speaker gives an order, makes a request, disagrees or makes a complaint. Politeness strategies are used to mitigate the force of such face-threatening acts.

Brown and Levinson identify four main strategies for carrying out a face-threatening act:

- do it directly without mitigation, i.e., what they call the 'bald on record' strategy;
- employ positive politeness strategies which seek to create a positive relationship with the hearer;
- employ negative politeness strategies which seek to minimise the intrusion;
- carry out the face-threatening act indirectly, 'off record', so that if there is any opposition from the hearer, the speaker can claim that no face-threatening act was intended.

## 8.3 The corpus

Email discussion lists provide a forum for asynchronous discussion about a specified field or theme. Those who wish to participate add their names to a list; they can then send messages to and receive messages from the list. Everyone on the list automatically receives copies of all messages sent to the list. The list chosen for study was Megabyte University (MBU-L), and the sample consisted of 23 consecutive messages posted to the list on 8 and 9 May 1995. Megabyte University was a fairly homogenous group composed mainly of university teachers of computers and writing. The tone of the messages in the sample is friendly. There is a strong group feeling, and although there can be disagreement, there is rarely hostility.

The discourse of email discussions was chosen as our focus because here the entire communication process is carried out by email. In other situations participants might use a mixture of media (Murray, 1988), but for most of the participants in email discussion lists, email will be the only form of communication which they have with other members of the group.

## 8.4  Face-threatening acts

It is in the nature of discussion groups that they are constantly generating situations that one or more of the participants might find in some way threatening. Naturally in discussions there will be disagreement, because if everyone agreed there would be little to discuss. Yet disagreement is potentially threatening. There will be the asking for and giving of advice, because this is a major function of such groups and participants often want help with specific problems. But this too can be threatening because it sets up a low power role for the one who asks for the information or advice, and a high power role for the one who gives the information or advice.

It is precisely this kind of threatening situation that Brown and Levinson focus on in their work. In many ways email discussions create the kinds of situations that we find in spoken discourse - participants need to make invitations and requests, to intrude upon another's (virtual) space, to disagree and to offer advice without undermining the standing of another participant. The participants may never see each other, but their 'face' is real enough.

There are three factors that contribute to the seriousness of a face-threatening act:

- the 'social distance' between speaker and hearer
- the 'relative power' of speaker and hearer
- the 'absolute ranking ... of impositions in a particular culture' (Brown and Levinson 1987, p.74).

For the purposes of this analysis, we will assume that all participants are of equal status and social distance. We cannot know their actual status from the sample, but we do know that most of the participants are university teachers, and although some may be more advanced in their profession than others, the evidence from within the sample indicates that they are functioning as a group of peers. We will also make no judgement about the ranking of the impositions found within the sample, as this depends very much on individual perception: some participants may be incensed by a cross-posting which leaves three copies of the same message in their mail boxes, while others may see this as trivial; some participants may feel threatened by advice, while others may welcome it.

However, the concept of relative power *is* significant here. When participants choose to respond to a request for information or support, they are presenting themselves as authorities on that subject. They, by their own evaluation, have the knowledge or experience needed to help the questioner. Therefore, within the context of the current segment of the discussion, they have assumed high-power rôles (although at other times they might take a low-power rôle by asking for advice themselves).

## 8.5  Politeness in written discourse

The original work by Brown and Levinson investigated politeness strategies in spoken discourse, and almost all of the politeness studies which followed their work have also focused on spoken discourse. However, a few researchers have successfully applied the politeness framework to written discourse. Myers (1989) identifies politeness strategies in non-interactive scientific articles. Hagge and Kostelnick (1989), investigating the use of politeness strategies in auditors' suggestion letters, find widespread use of negative strategies, achieved mainly by the use of passive constructions, nominalisations and hedges. Graham and David (1996), investigating 'non-routine memos' also find strategies which are mostly negative, mainly indirectness, tentativeness and indebtedness. These studies demonstrate that politeness strategies are indeed found in written text, and that the strategies identified tend, as in spoken discourse, to be predominantly negative strategies.

The many writers who have discussed violations of accepted behaviour, such as flaming, or have given guidelines for how to behave on the net, (Angell and Heslop, 1994) could be said to have discussed the issue of politeness in email. Such writers do not in general explicitly relate their discussions to Brown and Levinson's work on language. However, one paper which does make a clear link with Brown and Levinson's work is Herring (1994). Herring was investigating flaming and in particular the perception that men flame more than women. She found that positive and negative politeness strategies were used 'in roughly equal proportions' (p.284), but that women used politeness strategies (both positive and negative) far more frequently than men. This does not match my own findings for Megabyte University, but the difference could have arisen from the difference in the data used in the two studies. Herring was investigating lists in which flaming did occur, whereas the current study investigates a discussion which was chosen because the interaction was successful and flame-free.

## 8.6 Two messages

My investigation shows that participants in the sample make frequent use of politeness strategies and by so doing ensure the smooth running of the group. Their use of politeness strategies can be illustrated by an analysis of two messages. The first message is from S, a university teacher of English, who has used email discussion in one of his courses and has received negative feedback about this from his students. He is asking whether other people have had similar problems. This topic generated much interest. It was followed by 15 more messages on the same subject in the sample. The second message is a response to S by N.

### Message 1: topic initiation by S

I just got back my evaluations for the class I taught this last
semester, a class called Great Ideas, which is sort of a hybrid
of a 'Western Civ' class.  You can see the WWW page I used to
teach that class at: [www address]

Anyway, the student evaluations were an unusually mixed bunch for
me this semester, reflecting a pretty mixed bunch of students as
well.  One of the ways that was most 'mixed' was on participating
on the class listserv.  I think about a third of the evaluations
explicitly say something positive about using email in class,
while about half of them really did not like it at all and said
so.  I've used listservs in other classes with somewhat happier
results — usually there are two or three students out of 25 who
complain about it, but most (if they have an opinion at all)
usually say something like 'I didn't like this at first, but by
the end of the semester, I thought it was good idea.'

I guess what I'm trying to ask here is the classic student
evaluation question:  to what extent should I pay attention to
these negative reviews of email?  When these negative reviews
say participating on the listserv was 'too much work' (I
required two posts a week — one 'original' post about something
we've read or talked about in class, one 'response' post to
something someone else said), should I believe them? Have we
all perhaps been a wee bit too rosy about how wonderful and
positive the use of email listservs and discussion groups as a
means of extending the boundaries of the classroom?  In other

```
words, is there anyone else out there who has gotten some 'bad
reviews' of their own when it comes to incorporating computers
and computer networks into the classroom? Or do I just have a
particularly whiny bunch of students ;) ?

S
```

In the very first sentence of this message we can see positive politeness at work. S feels no need to justify talking about teaching, but assumes a shared interest in it. He does not explain the system of 'student evaluations', which he also assumes his audience will know about. He uses in-group language when he refers to the 'Western Civ' class, and clearly expects his audience to understand and use this reference in order to interpret the 'Great Ideas' class. He claims shared interest again by offering the address of the web page that he used for his class. By telling the readers 'You can see' this page he is indicating that he expects at least some of the audience to be sufficiently interested to follow this up.

So far there have been no face-threatening acts at all, but the writer has already used some positive politeness strategies. This is in keeping with Brown and Levinson's findings that while negative strategies are normally tied to a specific face-threatening act, positive strategies can be more free-standing, setting up a relationship between the participants which will serve to mitigate any face-threatening acts which may arise.

The second paragraph is an account of the problem, with more positive politeness in the form of colloquialism, 'pretty mixed bunch', and in-group language — 'listserv' is computer software which runs an email discussion list.

The third paragraph begins with the negative strategy of hedging, i.e. using a word or phrase that is used to soften the force of what is said. The writer uses a cogitative, 'I guess', followed by further hedging, 'I am trying to ask', instead of simply asking the question. By using tentativeness in this way he is softening the force of the question, and softening the requirement on other participants to respond. But immediately after this we return to positive strategies: in-group language ('listserv'), and colloquialism ('wee bit too rosy').

In the fourth paragraph there is more positive politeness in the form of colloquialism ('whiny'), informal syntax in the sentence-initial 'Or', and humour. There is also a 'smiley', and while smileys cannot occur in spoken conversation the use of this one does seem to be equivalent to using in-group language, and members of the group would be expected to interpret it correctly.

## Message 2: response from N

```
S writes:
[stuff deleted]
> extending the boundaries of the classroom?  In other words,
> is there anyone else out there who has gotten some 'bad
> reviews' of their own >    when it comes to incorporating
> computers and computer networks into the classroom?
```

Yep, I've gotten those bad reviews.  And it seems to me that I learned a lot from paying attention to them.  I'm not ready to give up on email.  But it does seem that we can't count on the generic student for whom one size fits all.  Some people do not want to have their boundaries extended.  Some want the classroom to stay in one place and not challenge them. I listen to those students, but I don't necessarily do what they want. Some students have complaints that cause me to rethink how I am doing something.  And sometimes all you can say is: 'Well at least I gave them a chance to try it.'  What did you think you would get from them?  What did you expect they would say about how it worked?  How did you think it worked?

N

In her reply, N begins by referring explicitly to S's message, and quoting from it (the angle brackets indicate quotation from another message). However, just before the quotation, N uses a positive politeness strategy, employing colloquial language in 'stuff deleted'. Clearly this is a factual comment — N has quoted some but not all of S's message — but she could have expressed it differently. If she had said 'several lines deleted' it would have carried a similar informational content, but would not have expressed positive politeness. By using the colloquial word 'stuff' she is indicating an informal relationship.

After the quotation, N immediately and strongly identifies herself with S's position, 'Yep, I've gotten those bad reviews'. This is a very explicit positive politeness strategy claiming shared experience, and it is reinforced by the colloquial language. It is also followed immediately by the face-threatening act. N has strong opinions on this subject, but even in her expression of them she mitigates the threat to S's face. She begins the second sentence of this paragraph with informal syntax, 'And', followed by a hedge 'it seems to me'. The effect of the 'And' and the 'it seems to me' can been seen by looking at the effect of the sentence without them. If instead N had simply written 'I learned a lot from paying attention to them' she would have been taking a much more dominating stance. While N continues to explain her position, she continues to use positive strategies of informality, of sharing S's concerns and of showing interest in S.

The use of hedging in this message is interesting. Hedges are normally used in spoken conversation as a negative strategy to modify the force of an imposition (and thereby maintain or increase social distance). But occasionally Brown and Levinson found hedging used as a 'device in positive politeness... to make one's own opinion safely vague' (1987, p.116). It is in this way that hedging is used here - N is softening the strength of her opinion by saying 'It seems to me'. This happens repeatedly in the data. Time after time, writers use hedging as a positive strategy, to soften the impact of their advice and opinions. When participants offer advice, they assume a high-power role, and this is potentially very threatening to the face of the recipient. By using hedging as a *positive* strategy to soften the force of their opinions, they are reducing the difference in relative power between the giver and receiver of the advice. The remarkably frequent use of this particular strategy seems to be a significant factor in the successful functioning of this group.

## 8.7 The wider sample

These two messages demonstrate how participants can successfully negotiate face-threatening acts through the use of a range of mainly positive politeness strategies. When we examine the data as a whole we find participants using strategies from all four of the categories identified by Brown and Levinson, although throughout the sample positive strategies predominate.

### Off record strategies

Off record strategies enable the speaker to carry out a face-threatening act indirectly, and are often used to enable speakers to avoid the responsibility of making the face-threatening act. One way in which off-record strategies can be realised is by over-generalisation. In the sample, this technique is used when a writer quotes another source as a means of giving advice: 'Mistake #4: Teachers believe they ought to tell students what they think it is important to know.' The writer does not say that the previous participant has made a mistake, and if challenged would have a way out - the quotation did not refer to this participant specifically but to teachers in general.

There are not many examples of indirect strategies in the data - perhaps because it is necessary to be more explicit in writing than in speech. The instances of off record strategies which do occur are mostly in the form of rhetorical questions which are used to give advice indirectly. For example, 'Do you use any variation of a portfolio system?' is really a strong suggestion that the reader *ought* to be using a portfolio system. Such rhetorical questions are not in general used to defer to the recipient or to allow the writer to back away from an imposition; instead, they mitigate a face-threatening act from a (temporarily) more powerful participant.

### Negative strategies

Negative politeness strategies relate directly to the hearer's need for freedom from imposition. They are what society in general normally understands by politeness. They show deference or minimise the imposition, and they have the effect of increasing or maintaining social distance.

In the sample negative strategies include occasional use of conventional politeness, for example 'Sorry for the cross-posting, folks'. Here the writer is apologising because people who belong to more than one list might receive more than one copy of this message. However, in the same sentence 'folks' is a positive strategy which is working to reduce the distancing effect of the apology. Coupland *et al* (1988) note that Brown and Levinson do not believe that strategies can be 'mixed' (Brown and Levinson, 1987, p.17), but just as Coupland *et al* found 'overlapping sets of face-related strategies' in spoken discourse (1988, p.255), the current study reveals a rich interplay of strategies within individual messages.

Hedging is used frequently. In spoken discourse this is usually a negative strategy, but, as discussed in the 'Two messages' section, in this sample hedging is normally used in a positive way to soften the force of the speaker's opinion and consequently decrease the relative power of the participants.

There are instances of minimising the imposition, for example, 'Just a suggestion'. Like the positive hedging described above, these are used to soften the force of the speaker's advice, and so have a certain positive effect. This example also includes ellipsis, a positive strategy, again demonstrating the use of a mixture of strategies to mitigate a single face-threatening act. There are a few instances of the negative strategy of giving deference - speakers deprecate their abilities, 'Someone who taught one of these classes is on this list and might ... respond better than I am', or suggest that they are to blame, 'Maybe the fault is with me...'. Yet these too are being used by speakers to minimise their own importance and so reduce relative power.

## *Positive strategies*

Positive strategies relate directly to the hearer's need to be liked and valued, and they create a positive relationship with the hearer by claiming common opinions, attitudes and knowledge, or by praising or agreeing with the hearer. They have the effect of reducing social distance between the participants. But positive strategies are also risky - they imply a degree of familiarity which could cause offence, and for this reason their use in society is relatively limited. It is therefore remarkable that by far the greatest number of politeness strategies found in this sample fall into the positive category. Positive strategies are varied and widespread, and greatly exceed negative strategies, both in quantity and variety.

Time and again a writer will express interest and give compliments such as 'This is an interesting question', 'I think E— makes an interesting point when he says...', 'I think this is a great idea!'. Often a writer will claim 'in-group membership' by using first names or nicknames, by using familiar language or in-group jargon such as 'Your friend and netdreg', 'Back to dissing ARRGH'. Within this category, Brown and Levinson identify the sub-strategy of 'contraction and ellipsis'. This too is widespread in the sample, 'Want to learn more...?', 'The moral of the story?'.

There are instances of the positive strategies of seeking agreement and avoiding disagreement - 'I agree with E—'s points...', 'True, though I believe...', 'I appreciate your post a great deal and by and large agree with it, but...'. When a writer wishes to contradict another participant, it seems to be considered particularly important within the group either to say something positive about the other participant, or to find an area of agreement, or at least to avoid overt disagreement. This is perhaps one of the key reasons why this group functions in a generally harmonious way - disagreements are handled 'politely' and do not normally lead to conflict.

Positive hedging has been discussed above in the 'Two messages' section. In the sample there are many examples of hedges used in this positive way, for example, 'I think it was relatively successful', where the double hedges of 'think' and 'relatively' are used to modify the writer's claim to success. It is clearly considered necessary that when participants take a high power role, they should mitigate the authority of their stance by using positive hedges.

There are several instances of asserting common ground, for example, 'I tried something like you suggest below with my class this semester'. There are instances of jokes, of showing appreciation of the other person's concerns, of making offers and promises, of being optimistic.

Brown and Levinson state that positive politeness is often general, expressing an interest in the hearer which may not necessarily be followed by a face-threatening act, whereas negative politeness relates to a particular face-threatening act. But while some positive strategies in the sample are used to create a positive atmosphere, many do relate to specific face-threatening acts, and we often find, for example, a compliment immediately before a disagreement or a positive hedge accompanying a piece of advice.

### Bald on record

Finally, the face-threatening act can be bald on record, that is, made directly, without mitigation. An example from the data is 'Write to me and I'll try to help'. This kind of strategy can be used in an emergency, or when there is a power difference between the speaker and the hearer, for example when a teacher is talking to a child or when the imposition is against the speaker, which is what we have here. In the data, we also find bald on record which demonstrates an informal and easy relationship between participants, as in 'Oh stop it, E—!'. This example forms part of a humorous exchange, and is combined in the same message with the positive strategy of joking. As one might expect, there are very few instances of bald on record strategies. Most of those which do occur tend to strengthen the group — an invitation, an imposition on the speaker, a joke — rather than realise a power differential.

## 8.8. Conclusion

In this short sample from Megabyte University, we can observe the successful negotiation of several face-threatening acts - requests, invitations, criticism, disagreement and advice. This is achieved mainly through the use of a wide range of positive politeness strategies. There are some instances of other types of strategy but these too are often used in a 'positive' way - bald on record to demonstrate a closeness expressed by insult humour, negative strategies to minimise the writer's authority, and off-record strategies to give advice without appearing to impose it. This indicates that the boundaries between the different types of politeness strategies are not always as clear cut as Brown and Levinson suggest, a finding which is supported by the frequent mixing of strategies in the data, where different kinds of strategies may be used to mitigate one face-threatening act.

We find positive politeness used in the way described by Brown and Levinson, to create a generally positive atmosphere rather than to mitigate a specific face-threatening act. This is achieved by the use of informality, in-group language and the expression of shared interests. However, in contrast to Brown and Levinson, we also find positive strategies directed at specific face-threatening acts, particularly when a participant wishes to express disagreement or give advice. When disagreeing, writers assert agreement or express interest in the points made by the previous participant before expressing their disagreement. When giving advice, writers use strategies such as positive hedging to soften the force of their authority and so reduce the relative power between themselves and the recipient. This enables participants to exchange ideas in a non-threatening manner, a factor which is critically important for a discussion group where disagreement and advice are necessary but must not lead to hostility which might threaten the existence of the group.

We conclude that Brown and Levinson's framework can usefully be applied to email discourse. The analysis shows that the use of politeness strategies is widespread in this discussion group. The many instances reinforce each other, promoting discussion in a safe atmosphere and acting to strengthen the group.

## Acknowledgement

The author would like to thank the writers of the two messages for permission to print and use them in this paper.

# 9. Effects of group identity on discussions in public on-line fora

Heather Matthews

## 9.1 Introduction

In a few decades computer connectivity has grown from a technical interest for a few specialists servicing academic and business needs to a heavily-marketed communication concept aimed at the general public.

Newt Gingrich (1995), Speaker of the US House of Representatives, is reported to have said 'Cyberspace is the Land of Knowledge', creating a vivid image of information readily accessible world-wide.  His is a vision of Cyberspace as a virtual library where visitors are engaged in exchanges of information necessary to plan or execute the work-related tasks. In contrast, Rheingold (1993) relates a tale of Cyberspace servicing emotional and recreational needs, with interactional dialogues providing social chatter.

This notion of the Internet as a medium which can support both work-related and social interactions forms the background for the study reported in this chapter. We describe a study of the activity on two public on-line conferencing fora, one aimed at computer professionals and the other with a New Age focus, which was undertaken to analyse the types of exchange in each of the groups. Whether they are transactional or interactional, all the dialogues on the fora studied are freely created by the participants.  As a medium, online conferencing is content free, being constructed by the dialogues that the members create. When Coulthard (1977, p. 80) discusses the motivation for conversations, stating that '.... it is a basic assumption of all except chance encounters that the person who initiates the encounter has some reason for doing so', he does not preclude purely social reasons.  The communication need of the fora members could be purely social, or it could be that they are seeking information.   This study examined dialogues in two fora, anticipating that the forum with an external focus would concentrate more on information exchange, and therefore contain more transactional dialogue, and the forum exploring an abstract emotional concept would contain more interactional dialogue.  In both cases it was expected that the content of fora dialogues would match the communication intentions of fora members.

## 9.2 Background

The following section considers background concepts important for the interpretation of the evidence in the study, beginning with some aspects that differentiate the public subscription computer-mediated communication (CMC) fora from the workplace or experimental CMC group.  Frey (1988, p.566) suggests some crucial differences between natural and contrived groups:

> When people choose to enter and remain in a group voluntarily, the group cannot rely on external forces for its existence; instead members must find ways to create and sustain the group.  Such groups must work hard to construct an identity that sustains members' passions; their survival depends on the success of these efforts.

This is particularly relevant for CMC groups where the participants are paying to use the system.  Unless their communication needs are met the individuals are unlikely to continue generating dialogues. In transactional dialogues, exchanges of information justify language production, but the purpose of interactional language production is less easily understood, and possibly more intriguing.

The construction and presentation of self is one answer - in considering why people exercise their language abilities Dennett (1991) suggests the construction of 'self' for the individual human as being the product of a web of words and deeds, leading to his assertion that 'you are what you speak'.  This human ability to use language to construct identities is exercised naturally throughout the course of our everyday interactions and there is no reason to suppose that computer mediated interactions should lack this imperative.  Berger and Luckmann (1967) recognise the importance of conversation in  the 'social construction of reality', a concept that Jones (1995) believes has been overlooked in many of the contrived, task-based, examinations of CMC usage.  Indeed the intentions behind dialogues on commercial CMC networks may even have been misunderstood by the service providers themselves.  Carpenter (1983, cited in Baym, 1995, p.9) observes that 'what CompuServe apparently didn't realize when they first put together their potpourri of consumer goods is that people are not crying out for airline schedules and biorhythms, but to talk to one another'.  Whether they are exchanging information or sharing realities, people appear to need communication with others.

This need to communicate with each other has been demonstrated in the past by the proliferation of the household telephone.  Research to ascertain reasons for the use of the household telephone measured two factors that are relevant to this study: sociability and instrumentality (Dimmick, Sikan and Patterson, 1994).  Interactional dialogues support sociability, and transactional dialogues support instrumentality. Dimmick *et al*. found a balance in telephone use, with users who reported high gratification for sociability having a corresponding low for instrumentality, and vice versa.

Literacy is a prerequisite to CMC but writing is more than just another way of producing language, it offers the human an opportunity to off-load memories.  Putting memories into the external environment creates the potential for literate societies to evolve what Dennett (1991) called a different 'virtual architecture' for their cognitive processing.

Another difference that literacy appears to encourage is a perspective on language focused on *form* rather than on *content*. Ellis and Beattie (1993)  argue that it is the immutability of written language that drives the writer to deliberate long and hard over the choice of words. Gist is not the issue; they are searching for what sounds (or perhaps, looks) best. When technology is introduced to language production some transformation occurs. Ong (1982) uses the term 'self-consciously informal' to describe electronically recorded interviews - they are spoken language but do not sound as any previous speech would. Text-based conversations may assume characteristics not observed in spontaneous spoken dialogues and with this process will come gains and losses. Some may consider online conferencing as merely a refinement and extension of telephone communication, with which we feel a degree of familiarity. However this may not be the case, as the two systems are closer in technology than psychology. Both differ from other traditional media in that they are empty of content and their uses must be created wholly by the user (Dimmick *et al.*, 1994). However, in the creation of that content, users are moving from orality, that all human beings are born into, to literacy and the technology of writing, which is completely culturally constructed (Ong, 1982).

## 9.3. Study One

### Method

In the first study, transcripts of two separate one hour synchronous conferences from each of two fora 'The Computer Professionals Forum' and 'The New Age Forum' were collected and analysed in terms of the speech acts they represented. Two types of speech act, transactional and interactional, were identified and used in the study. The Computer Professionals Forum served as an example of a concrete-focus forum, while the New Age Forum was chosen as an example of a forum with an abstract emotional focus.

In addition to this analysis, a qualitative content analysis was carried out, looking particularly for socially-oriented aspects of the discussions.

## Results

The main hypothesis of this study required the transactional and interactional dialogue to be compared. Transactional dialogue showed a statistically significant difference between the two fora in the predicted direction ($t = 2.163$, d.f.= 1,70; $p<0.05$), i.e. the Computer Professionals Forum discussions contained more transactional acts than the New Age Forum discussions. Interactional dialogue also showed a statistically significant difference in the predicted direction ($t = 2.000$, d.f.= 1,70; $p<0.05$).

Both fora contained comments to support the assumption that participants were in cohesive groups. The following is a particularly striking example of group solidarity both for its expression and its content (participants are numbered for ease of reference):

### New Age Forum

```
1:    Teb, Chole wants to know our mantra
2:    Tell her, some others may not know it
1:    Chole, We're right and the rest of the world is wrong!!!!
```

```
3:   I'm Right and the rest of the world is wrong!!
4:   I'm Right and the rest of the world is WRONG!!
5:   I'm Right and the rest of the world is wrong
1:   It's a very positive mantra Chole
```

Rather than just accepting the filtering out of social cues, participants added comments (in italics in the examples) to describe actions and emotions in support of their contributions, and in response to contributions from others, a textual version of the emoticons used in some email interactions or perhaps a reflection of the textual structures used in MUDs and MOOs. For example:

### Computer Professional Forum
```
1:   Hows Terry doing with WinCim2 (noticing he isn't here)
```

### New Age Forum
```
1:   Oh, but she wasn't running off killing people over
     imaginary boundaries (snort)
```

### New Age Forum
```
1:   Let me offer a few facts.  In England, before the Norman
     conquest
2:   (listening)
```

## Computer Professional Forum
```
1:   Paul, you going to the Chorleywood meet?
2:   I won't be in London unfortunately (sob)
```

This last example, as well as adding another dimension to the message by the addition of the 'sob' annotation, also mentions a real-life meeting, suggesting that the participants also meet outside the online forum.

Participants gave no impression of living in a fantasy world or of experiencing a total absorption that took them out of their physical environments. Comments were made that invited the Cybercommunity to share their reality, for example:

### Computer Professional Forum
```
1:   Baby's crying again, wife's asking me to mind the baby.
2:   I'm trying to keep an eye on Frost on TV
3:   My other half is watching TV, three labradors are fast
asleep
```

### New Age Forum
```
1:   It sure is hard to type while eating BBQ ribs and a kitty
     sitting on your mousepad purring
```

## Discussion

The purpose of this study was to provide naturalistic research into two different fora types. The first conclusion to be drawn from the data presented here is that the results support the initial hypothesis, since the forum with an external focus (Computer Professionals) did contain more transactional dialogue, while the forum exploring an abstract emotional concept (New Age Forum) generated more interactional dialogue.

However, what was also clear from these results is that the Computer Professionals forum contained high levels of social dialogue, while the New Age Forum offered transactional exchanges. Much of the dialogue on both fora consisted of casual conversation, confirming Carpenter's assertion that people just want to talk to one another. In the case of on-line CompuServe conferences, participants are paying for their talk, giving a strong indication that such talk is valued. The talk may not be regarded as functionally valuable, in the way that goal-directed computer-mediated communication might be valued in the context of a project or task; rather it is valuable because it satisfies a basic human need for communication.

The high levels of interactional activity in both groups indicate that participants are prepared to invest time in this aspect of their dialogues. It may be that in the absence of other cues, participants need to develop some 'feel' for who they are in dialogue with in order to give credibility to any exchange.

The dialogues indicating a desire to augment text with scanned images or face-to-face meetings suggests that some participants are using the medium as an additional communication channel to support conventional social interaction, rather than a replacement. This behaviour does not fit the pattern suggested by other research (Rheingold, 1993; Turkle, 1996), which show cybercommunities consisting of consciously-constructed pseudo-identities, with 'life on the screen' regarded as an alternative, rather than an adjunct, to real life.

## 9.4  Study Two

### Method

In the second study of the same fora, a questionnaire was used to measure the participants' own perceptions of their goals in using the fora in question. Subjects were recruited from the population of CompuServe members who responded to requests for help posted in the 'New Age Forum' with 19 responses, and the 'Computer Professionals Forum' with 27 responses. The requests were posted immediately prior to commencement of the target conferences.

The first section of the questionnaire contained a 15 item scale that measured respondents' perceived communication intention for sociability and instrumentality. The second section requested personal data, which was also analysed.

## Results

### Communication Intention

The ratios for transactional and interactional speech acts, obtained in Study One, were compared with the reported instrumentality and sociability gathered via the questionnaires.

Ratios for transactional dialogue generated and also for instrumentality reported were both higher for the Computer Professionals Forum. However, the Computer Professionals ratio for transactional dialogue (41.0), was only 8.3 per cent higher than the New Age Forum ratio (39.6), whereas the reported Computer Professionals Forum instrumentality ratio was 26.9 per cent higher, with 69.3 reporting an instrumental reason for participating in the conference, compared with 49.2 for the New Age Forum.

In contrast, ratios for both the interactional dialogue generated and sociability reported were higher for the New Age Forum. For interactional dialogue the New Age Forum ratio (62.4) was only 5.4 per cent higher than the Computer Professionals ratio (59.0), whereas for reported sociability the ratio was 35.6 per cent higher, with 50.8 of New Age Forum members citing sociability as their motive for participating in the conference compared with 32.7 of Computer Professionals.

### Biographical data

The personal data gathered via the questionnaire showed that membership of the fora differed on sex, nationality and age group, presenting a number of potential confounding variables.

All the New Age Forum members were female, whereas the majority, (89 per cent), of Computer Professionals Forum members were male. All the New Age Forum were US nationals, whereas UK nationals were predominant in the Computer Professionals (81 per cent), with a number of US replies (15 per cent), and one Canadian (4 per cent). The data on age groups shows another difference between the groups, with all the Computer Professionals being in the 18-30 age group whereas the majority of the New Age Forum members (74 per cent) were 31-50.

### Discussion

The purpose of the second study was to examine the relationship between the content of the fora dialogues and the communication intention of the members. The perceived intentions reported by members did support the original hypothesis examined in Study One. Members of the forum with a concrete external focus, Computer Professionals, intended more information-based, transactional, conferencing, while members of the forum exploring a more abstract, emotional, concept intended to have more interactional dialogues.

However, when intentions were compared with performance, results were not consistent for both fora. Computer Professionals members reported that their online conferencing activities were more concerned with information transactions than social interactions. New Age Forum members reported their activities as more balanced between information transactions and social interactions. Although the fora members perceived their intentions differently these perceptions did not translate into performance and content of the online dialogues did not reflect the differentiation predicted by the perceptions reported. The content of the Computer Professionals Forum dialogues did not match the reported communication intention of the members, in that the proportion of socially-oriented messages in this group was almost the same as that in the New Age Forum (CP59.0 compared to NA62.4, despite only a ration of 32.7 of Computer Professionals members reporting sociability as their motive for participating in the forum) whereas the New Age Forum had a closer match between dialogue content and reported intentions.

The similarity of members' biographical data may suggest a basis for the apparent stability of the New Age Forum which appears to have created a cybercommunity that will generate dialogues that satisfy the communication intentions of its members.

## 9.5 Conclusion

This research had two main purposes:
- to examine the content of dialogues generated in public fora;
- to consider how these dialogues satisfied the communication needs of the participants.

Study One examined dialogue content and reported that the forum with an external focus did concentrate more on information exchange, and the forum exploring an abstract emotional concept did contain more interactional dialogue. Two other issues of further interest were identified as:
- the use of multiple context spaces;
- the desire for supplementary communication channels.

Each issue contains elements of interest to social psychologists and further research is needed to gain a fuller understanding of these new human activities.

One group maintained multiple context spaces throughout their conferences. This made the dialogues difficult to follow, and resulted in a public space populated by dyadic exchanges. However, when looked at as complete conference texts, rather than exchange by exchange, it can be seen that they hold a superficial resemblance to the action of many television dramas, or soaps - short sequences of dialogue with rapidly changing scenes, requiring the reader to hold in memory multiple open context spaces. For anyone first viewing a soap, without the shared history, scenes can be confusing and the dialogue dull. It is necessary to know the characters before meaning can be extracted from what appears to be mundane or trite. These conferences could be satisfying because they offer an opportunity to develop interactive online drama, living 'soaps'. When Baym (1995) reported on the uses of messages posted to Usenet, an extremely popular network, she identified the most popular newsgroup as that which carried gossip about soap operas. She found that in the message environment CMC could create a dynamic and rich community filled with social nuance and emotion. Synchronous conferences offer further opportunities for creation of social worlds.

The second issue was identified in all four conference texts examined. The fora members showed a desire for supplementary communication channels, and this could indicate that CMC is being used as an additional medium in their portfolio of social interaction skills. More research is needed to understand whether online dialogues are the communication medium of choice, or merely of convenience - whether CMC is satisfying or merely sublimating the human need for social interaction.

Study Two looked at the relationship between the content of the fora dialogues and the communication intention of the members. The differences we found between perceptions of communication intentions and performance could have been accounted for by gender differences. Males may be reluctant to admit their need for mere chat, and justify the investment in both the technology and the online subscription on instrumentality rather than sociability grounds. Although this research did not analyse dialogues for gender, the number of female respondents was unexpectedly high. Again, further research is needed to better understand whether men and women use the fora dialogues for different purposes. If there is a gender imbalance in levels or patterns of interactional use it could have the potential to create, or resolve, tensions involving levels of social interaction in real-life relationships.

There is little doubt that many in our society will enjoy using the new communication technologies, but others may be reluctant to communicate this way. Reluctant users may experience difficulty when education and workplace communication demands the use of CMC. Understanding more about the process of writing online dialogues will suggest strategies to overcome initial reluctance and encourage wider acceptance of the new medium. This study examined the effects of group identity on dialogues and found that both concrete and abstract emotional focus led to high levels of social interaction, possibly reflecting a need within society, rather than a demand created by service providers. This purely social interaction, what Argyle (1998) might call 'playfulness', could be an essential element of successful CMC.

# 10. Literal or Loose Talk: the negotiation of meaning on an internet discussion list

Sonja Launspach

## 10.1 Introduction

This paper presents the negotiation of meaning for a disputed term on the Internet list, Fasola, which discusses Shape Note (Sacred Harp) singing, an American hymnody tradition. The hypothesis argues that it is not a lack of context that requires the negotiation of the term in dispute, but the overabundance of contextual assumptions that participants bring to the interaction. The paper explores the rôles played in the dispute by this broadened context as well as by definitions of community.  First, the relevant theoretical concepts will be discussed; then the data analysis and concluding discussion will be presented.

## 10.2 Theoretical Background

### Mutual Knowledge

Sociologists debate the concept of mutual knowledge.  While there is disagreement over the possibility and of the definition of mutual knowledge, there is an agreement that some kind of shared knowledge is necessary for communication to take place. Schutz claims that speakers assume their knowledge of the world is not identical, but similar, which allows them to act as if they had identical experiences. Instead of actual knowledge, he argues, speakers maintain a set of idealisations about the world; one, that there is a common world and two, that while each individual has a separate experience of that 'world', for any interaction the participants select and interpret common objects in an identical manner or a manner that is sufficient for all practical purposes (Schutz, 1962). In other words, they agree on a shared perspective for the current interaction.

Sperber and Wilson (1986), on the other hand, approach the issue of mutual knowledge from a different point of view. They deny that true or complete mutual knowledge is possible between speakers. Instead they claim 'mutual manifestness' is required for communication. They define as 'manifest' in an interaction, that which might be perceivable or inferrable. Hearers make use of their cognitive environment, the set of mentally represented assumptions that are perceived or inferred, to interpret utterances.  One speaker's cognitive environment may intersect with another's when the same set of assumptions is manifest to both speakers. This overlap creates a mutual cognitive environment.

Some kind of shared perspective or mutual cognitive environment is necessary to coordinate social action, such as talk.  In conversation, speakers' turns can serve to check or display their understanding of the current shared perspective.  However, when speakers have selected different perspectives or have a different set of assumptions, communication breaks down. In the dispute on the Fasola list, a lack of intersection between the differing sets of assumptions associated with the term 'raunchy' contributes to the need to negotiate a common interpretation of the term, as well as to negotiate its applicability to Shape Note singing.

### Loose Talk

Another element relevant to the analysis is Sperber and Wilson's notion of 'loose use' of language, the everyday use of metaphoric or figurative language (1991).  In loose use, an utterance does not literally represent the state of affairs it describes. Instead, there is an 'interpretive resemblance'; that is, '… any object can be used to represent any other object it resembles' (Blakemore, 1992, p. 161).  An utterance is an interpretive representation to the degree that it resembles another in semantic and logical properties. Loose use can be an effective way to communicate propositions as long as the hearer has some way to select which logical and contextual implications the speaker intends to convey.

The hearer has the responsibility for identifying the appropriate contextual implications for an utterance; that is, the implication that represents the thought being communicated. Usually, the hearer derives the contextual implications of an utterance from the content of the utterance and the context (the cognitive environment).  Further, contextual implications may be strongly or weakly implicated.  Strong implicatures have tighter constraints on hearer's choices, while weak implicatures have fewer constraints on contextual assumptions. Loose or metaphoric use often conveys a range of partly strong, partly weak implicatures.

### Definitions of Community

On the list, the participants assume they have the Shape Note (SN) community in common. But what does it mean to be a part of a 'community' on the Internet? Licklider and Taylor (1968) speculate that communities on the Internet would be shaped by common interests rather than geographic space.  Stone (1991) elaborates on this idea, stating that virtual communities are collection points for the common beliefs and practices of people who are physically separated.  Instead of physical or geographic space, the Internet provides users with a 'socially produced space' as a basis for a community (Jones, 1995).

In the case of the Fasola discussion list, this is indeed a community that is geographically separated. Moreover, the list is often the single connection to the SN community that some participants have, since they live in places that do not have a SN singing group. Therefore, for many singers, the list provides an important connective function. However, Jones (1995, p.12) states that 'connection does not inherently make for community, nor does it lead to any necessary exchange of information, meaning or sense making at all'.  The assumption of a unified community is one of the notions that breaks down quickly in the data. In fact, the list members belong to several, often overlapping, communities. The first community is the list, which has its own norms and rules for interaction. Next, there is the idealised vision of the SN community, and the different musical backgrounds of the list participants.

The idealised view of the SN community contains elements that unite all singers of this music, such as the distinct harmonies, songs led from the middle of the open square, dinner on the grounds and the friendliness and welcome that practitioners extend to newcomers and old timers alike. In addition to the musical experience of the SN community, each participant brings their individual musical background and training to list interactions.

These different communities are not mutually exclusive, but the norms of each participant's community play an important role in the interpretation of interactions on the list, as is demonstrated by the participants in the dispute who draw on their 'common' knowledges for the contextual assumptions to recover an interpretation for the disputed utterance.

## 10.3   Methodology and Data Analysis

The data is taken from the Fasola discussion list of Shape Note or Sacred Harp music, a traditional style of hymn singing in four part harmony that is sung *a cappella*. The notes are written in different geometric shapes, representing intervals, rather than in the standard European musical notation.

The discussion of the meaning and applicability of the term 'raunchy' to SN music took place over a period of four days. There were a total of 41 messages in all, ranging in length from 4 - 121 lines, the average being 25 lines. There were a total of 23 participants, with 6 who posted 2 or more messages. These participants included 7 women, 13 men and 3 people whose gender was not immediately evident from their name. The discussion did not appear to be dominated by a few participants, since more than half of the messages, 24, were sent by individuals posting once. The primary objector to the term 'raunchy' posted 7 times and the original user of the term 3 times.

The topic thread developed as follows - the initial message with the disputed term 'raunchy' was posted, followed by a response objecting to the use of the term. Next, the original poster tried to explain the 'context' of his first message. At this point in the discussion, other participants had already begun to post their interpretation of the term, either in the original 'context' or just their own individual interpretation. The original objector posted dictionary definitions of the disputed terms (several others came into dispute along the way), as a means of supporting their claim. The original poster later sent a message that explicitly stated what the term implied for him in relation to SN music. Other messages, both pro and con, were posted, some of which degenerated into name calling and professional and class-based insults. At the end, other participants stepped in, both to move the discussion away from the disputed terms and to enforce the list standards of conduct.

One difficulty of designing turns, that is, writing posts for Internet discussion lists is the problem of recipient design. In addition to any intended recipient, there are also the ratified overhearers, those who are not presently participating in the topic thread, but who normally post messages; and the lurkers, those who seldom or never post messages on any topic. In this instance, a ratified overhearer, GH, responds to the post, outside of the context of the original topic, which was the discussion of a Compact Disk, and derives a negative connotation for the term. GH's objection to the use of 'raunchy' laid the groundwork for the negotiation of the interpretation of this term by the list participants. GH relies on the semantic properties of 'raunchy' to infer a negative implication for its use in FP's post. FP, on the other hand, appears to have intended a figurative use for the term. The list participants' different backgrounds and different musical community memberships influence the interpretive representations derived for the utterance, focusing on the term itself.

The two posts that started the dispute are given below. The disputed term, 'raunchy' was first used in the context of a description of a Compact Disk of American folk songs in response to a previous poster's question.

### The original post
```
I was originally turned on to S.H. [Sacred Harp] music in 1964
by my teacher [name omitted] of blessed memory.  [name
omitted], every inch the Harvard man, loved the raunchy part
writing. (emphasis added: S.L.)
```

### The initial response by GH
```
Is anyone else getting *really* tired of this?
Its not 'raunchy' part writing.
[name omitted] its not 'crunchy' harmonies.
its not 'earthy, humble, close-to-the mud music'.
If you all want to go slumming, I suggest you find a nice slum
somewhere to do it in. Sacred Harp *isn't* it.
```

### FP's response to GH's post
```
[parts of GH's post  text-copied—omitted here]

I was surprised by the angry & confrontational tone of this
posting

My point was... that different people loved and valued this
music, from different perspectives and different places in life
and career.
```

The response of the original poster, FP, to GH shows that GH mistook the intended interpretation of the term, at least from FP's point of view. The discussion could, of course, have ended with FP's clarification of the context for his use of 'raunchy', but it did not, in part because GH continued to dispute the appropriateness of the term for SN music. GH based their reasons for their interpretation on two things - the encoded meaning of 'raunchy', (posting dictionary definitions to be perfectly clear) and the musical community membership of FP.

The issue of community membership plays an important role in the negotiation of the 'correct' interpretation of the term for GH and the other participants who begin to contribute to the topic thread. Since intonation, tone of voice, gesture or facial expression are all absent clues that a physical setting would provide, the resources which participants have for constraining their contextual assumptions are limited. This lack of nonverbal, but essential, conversational signals is recognised by participants on the Internet. Research has shown that numerous compensatory strategies have been invented; for instance, the use of parenthetical expression to clarify utterances (Launspach, 1994). On this list, participants have only their mental encyclopaedias, memories and experiences to bring to the interpretation of the message, with their musical community membership and experiences of SN singing as the most salient.

The posts of the other list participants are divided between those who interpreted the term positively, like FP; those who interpreted it negatively, like GH; and those who tried to maintain humour and list norms. Many responses also included other descriptive terms that were incorporated into the topic thread ('crunchy', 'slumming' and 'earthy'). The following sections provide examples of each of these perspectives.

The list participants who derived a positive interpretation for the term(s) use several tactics:

- they widen or loosen the interpretive representation of the word;
- they defend its use based on personal experience/opinion or its use by a SN authority/old-timer;
- they select a different term to define as pejorative, the term 'slumming'.

In order to clear up the dispute, FP posts an explanation of the intended meaning of 'raunchy' in this context. The following examples show support for FP's interpretation of the disputed term; (c) is FP's explanation.

```
(a). Why, oh why, do we need to accuse others of 'slumming'
when we take issue with their aesthetic stance?'Crunchy' and
'raunchy' are adjectives used quite frequently in the most
enthusiastic tones to describe *positive* attributes of non-
classical-Western music.
```

```
(b). it's clear that the adjective [raunchy] was not
pejorative. Such terms and even 'funky' have been used as terms
of approval in describing vernacular psalmody…' 'I'll say
again, the term 'slumming' is clearly pejorative, and sheds
more heat than light on the subject.'
```
(c). FP's post.
```
I admit that the word'raunchy'has pejorative connotations
```

```
(though not to me) — to me it has connotations of sensuality
and unconventionality… Sorry for the possible misunderstanding.

But none of us around here are'slumming,'to the best of my
knowledge.'
```

On the other hand, there is the perspective that the term is deliberately pejorative to SN music. This interpretation seems to be based on a more literal reading of the semantic content of the word as evidenced by the posting of dictionary definitions in support for this side of the dispute. The definitions were text-copied by others on both sides of the dispute or used humorously in an attempt to diffuse the argument. The following are excepts from posts which interpreted the term negatively.

```
(a). 'I continue to find disgusting in the extreme the so-far-
unanimous outpouring of people who find the term'raunchy'to be
an accurate description of this music..'

(b). How can *a musical interval* be raunchy? Its like the
distance between a child's eyes.

(c). I've seen a lot of smoke blown from a lot of people trying
[to] redefine the word 'raunchy' to mean something nice. It
doesn't  wash. It doesn't mean anything nice.[FP] didn't mean
anything nice by it.
```

In addition to the term's 'meaning', the status of speakers was used as a means to support the intended interpretation of the word 'raunchy'. It is in this aspect of the negotiation that the differing musical community memberships on the list play a role in the ongoing disagreement over the appropriateness of the term's use. The presence of community membership in this topic thread is divided into two main uses - the personal membership of individual posters and the division between classical and folk music traditions. Participants use their knowledge of group membership and overlapping networks as well as the background of their personal music community(s) as a resource for deriving their interpretation of 'raunchy'.

   The following three categories describe the types of musical backgrounds for most of the participants on the list:
1. The traditional singer (without formal music training): one who grew up in a family or church that sings SN. Some singers come from families with a long tradition of SN singing. Most of the 'traditional singing families' are in the southern US or the Ozark mountains. This style of singing has a rhythmic pulse and a nasal quality. It is often used as the model and is considered by many to be the authentic sound for SN, even if individual groups do not emulate it in their own singing.
2. Singers with varying backgrounds in music, ranging from untrained to formally trained, who discovered this type of music as part of their participation in the folk

music revival. Singers with this background tend to sing the music more as it is written without the rhythmic pulse of the traditional Southern singing.
3. Classically trained or professional musicians who have discovered SN music, often through their connections to early music. Their approach is often more melodic and their voicing is more classical (i.e. European).

The different prestige that participants give to classical and folk music influences the view of this term as negative. Also, the group membership of the original poster plays a role in the conflict, since his membership in the classical music establishment is seen by some to contribute to his devaluing of SN music as evidenced by his use of 'raunchy' and contributes to the interpretation of the term as pejorative by one of the posters.

The following excerpt shows the references to musical community membership and its rôle in the interpretation, understanding and appreciation of SN, which, in turn, influence how one describes (or is allowed to describe) this music.

(a). —the tone of the remarks being so out of keeping with the spirit of the shape-note singing community and indeed of civil discourse upon a subject one shares with others a love for.

(b). For me, one of the best things about the Fasola list has been the diversity of experience that various members bring to the discussions of the music that we share and that we love. We all bring something different into the hollow square, and we all leave with something a little different afterwards. This has always been true: it's true in the traditional South, and it's even more true today, when the music has been embraced by many who came late to it.

The example below also shows the conflict between the classical and folk traditions.

(a). I'd also like to examine why people admire so the people who have sought to iron tidbits from the Sacred Harp repertoire flat of all redeeming social value & shoehorn them into the classical repertoire.

You have to respect the traditions music comes from; you have to have a feel for the elements you incorporate or take out. It can't just be an academic exercise.

The widespread acceptance of classical style, even by people who don't much like the actual *sound* of it, as somehow 'better', can have & has had a lethal effect on traditional singers everywhere in the world, not only in the Sacred Harp world.

In the end, it was the appeal to a different community membership that ended the discussion, that of the community of the list itself, a separate non-musical community. There was a reassertion of the list as the primary community of membership; the participants were reminded of their responsibility to this community and the need to maintain list norms for standards of conduct. This direction in the topic thread surfaces midway and continues until the end.  The following excerpts are examples of this aspect of the discussion.  The posts tended to be reminders of consequences for conduct beyond the list itself - the list is not a closed community, the possibility of interacting with list members in 'real-life,' and the desire for individuals to act responsibly toward others so that no imposition of the 'civility Police' by the list owner would occur.

```
(a). Your words may be read by people you sing with,
people you work with,
or people you have not met yet.

These discussions of ours are archived,
and available for perusal, and study, and recall,
not only in the Fasola archives,
but on computers here, and there, and all over.

Please think about what you are writing,
who will read it, what you mean to say,
and how you will feel about your words in the future,
for they may return to you when you least expect it.

(b). My own experience is that after hearing 'I know you from
the list' from lurkers met at singings, I usually think much
more carefully about what I say and how I say it. It has not
stopped me from speaking my mind when provoked, but it made me
very try to be careful about the way I worded it and to address
the offending sentiments not the person speaking.
```

This topic thread ended after the appeals to the standards of list norms prevailed and the list turned to the discussion of other topics.

## 10.4  Concluding discussion

This interaction has demonstrated some of the difficulties that participants encounter in deriving the intended interpretation for utterances in the contextual environment of Cyberspace. One difficulty is the ability of participants to perceive or infer the same or similar set of contextual assumptions, since Cyberspace does not contain all of the clues speakers normally rely on to derive the contextual implications for utterances. Another difficulty is determining whether the utterance should be interpreted solely on its encoded meaning, or on possible metaphoric / interpretive representations.

In this instance, GH did not derive FP's intended interpretation of the term 'raunchy'. GH's interpretation appears to be based on three factors - the content of the utterance, that is the semantic properties of the phrase containing the term; their own mental encyclopaedia, memories and experience; and the musical community membership of FP. Throughout the discussion, GH insisted on a pejorative interpretation for the term, despite the explanations by FP and the support of other participants, who also derived interpretations similar to FP's.

Normally, GH and the other participants would access from their cognitive environments contextual assumptions associated with propositions containing 'raunchy' and reject those that are not relevant. However, in this situation, contrasting views of the contextual implications of the utterance caused the use of the term 'raunchy' to come into dispute. It is clear in this discussion that GH misjudged the way the utterance was intended to be relevant, since the speaker, FP, later explicitly states that he intended an interpretive rather than literal representation of the term.

In this topic thread, and on discussion lists in general, what can be mutually manifest is limited by the technology of the Internet. Participants are restricted to the linguistic code and unable to use other resources normally available in conversations, such as the physical environment. This lack of other environmental clues causes a reduction of what can be perceived, but not necessarily what can be inferred. Thus, on the Internet, there are fewer resources for hearers to use to constrain which contextual assumptions to utilise to interpret an utterance. In a sense, then, there is *too much* contextual information used by participants on discussion lists to determine relevant contextual assumptions. This creates a greater chance for miscommunication.

This discussion thread highlights two difficulties faced by users of the Internet - firstly, the establishment of a mutual cognitive environment and secondly, the difficulty of determining the line between the literal and metaphoric use of words. While these difficulties in communication are not exclusive to the Internet, the Internet does provide researchers with a unique chance to explore the processes that speakers use to work out these problems.

# 11. Electronic Mail, Communication and Social Identity: a social psychological analysis of computer-mediated group interaction

Jacqueline Taylor

## 11.1 Introduction

Computer-mediated communication (CMC) systems are often used to link geographically separate individuals, allowing them to conduct group-based project work at a distance. However, it is unclear how using these systems affects some facets of group work. In 1990, Huber suggested that much of the theory for small group interaction needed to be re-examined in a computer-supported context. Since then, researchers have started to investigate whether the social psychological literature on group interaction can be used to understand computer-mediated group interaction (Adrianson and Hjelmquist, 1991). However, systematic research has rarely been conducted within *realistic* contexts; rather it has tended to study inexperienced participants in artificial situations. A second criticism of much of the research into CMC is that it frequently does not address the social interactions that occur within groups, but rather concentrates on the outcome of group work (Finholt *et al.*, 1990). There has been very little research on the way that CMC affects the way individuals perceive each other and the group, and the relationship between these perceptions and the style and content of communication. The remainder of this introduction will review research into the effects of CMC on group communication and interpersonal perception, the different theoretical explanations for the findings, and the rationale and hypotheses for the study reported here.

### Group communication

Using email for communication between group members has been shown to have a number of effects on the content and style of group discussion. In particular three effects have frequently been observed - flaming, self-disclosure and balance of participation.

Steele (1983) defines flaming as 'to speak incessantly and/or rabidly on some relatively uninteresting subject or with a patently ridiculous attitude'. A more recent definition of flaming is 'a message that uses derogatory, obscene or inappropriate language' (*Computer User's Dictionary*, 1994). It is not clear whether this move from a focus on 'incessant' communication to a focus on 'negative' language has been stimulated by changing norms within the computing sub-culture or an actual change in the way users are communicating. Early research consistently found flaming in computer-mediated group discussions (Sproull and Kiesler, 1984). Recently however, researchers have questioned the extent and nature of flaming. For example, in an extensive survey of articles on CMC, Lea, O'Shea and Fung (1991) found that despite many references to flaming, only a few of these were supported by empirical research. A further problem is that there is some confusion as to how flaming should be operationalised. Some studies include only language which is either extremely positive or negative (McCormick and McCormick, 1992), or which includes swearing and insults (Siegal *et al.*, 1986), while other studies use wider definitions. For example, Sproull and Kiesler (1984) include all messages conveying bad news, social (non-work) communication or 'paralanguage'.

Many researchers relate the use of email to a more open and informal style of language. In an early study, Kiesler and Sproull (1986) found that when they distributed a self-evaluation questionnaire by either paper or email, those participants replying by email reported more types of undesirable behaviour. More recently, email has been used to conduct sensitive surveys and counselling (Turkle, 1995). However, although many CMC studies have noted the occurrence of self-disclosure (McCormick and McCormick, 1992), this has not been systematically investigated. In contrast, self-disclosure has received much attention in the group processes literature conducted in face-to-face contexts. For example, Cathcart and Samovar (1992) suggest that our impact and influence on a group is partially determined by what personal information we disclose to other members of the group and how we disclose it. There needs to be investigation of the contexts under which self-disclosure takes place during computer-mediated discussion (for instance, whether anonymity is important).

During computer-mediated discussions there tends to be more balanced participation from group members, compared to face-to-face discussions. Dubrovsky, Kiesler and Sethna (1991) called this effect the 'equalisation phenomenon'. Huff and King (1988) explain the more balanced participation in email discussions between graduates and undergraduates in terms of the reduced status information, which enables the less dominant members (undergraduates) an opportunity to be 'heard'. Similarly, Siegal *et al.* (1986) found more balanced participation between males and females in email discussions and attribute this to the lack of information regarding participants' gender. However, it is unclear what impact social identity may have on group member participation.

## *Interpersonal perception*

The absence of social cues in CMC is widely hypothesised to affect interpersonal perception and result in the treatment of others, resulting in a depersonalised manner. For example, Sproull and Kiesler (1991) propose that the lack of cues in CMC creates the equivalent of 'a tribe of masked and robed individuals'. However, they collected no interpersonal data to substantiate this hypothesis. Perceptions of group members and of the group have received surprisingly little attention in the CMC literature. Within organisational psychology and the group processes literature, group cohesion (the feeling of unity among group members, of being closely knit) has been a major focus; however it has received virtually no attention in computer-mediated group research. Studies conducted with face-to-face groups have shown group cohesion to be important for a group to be effective and for members to enjoy their experience together (Elias, Johnson and Fortman, 1989). Without group cohesion, individual members are unlikely to commit themselves to the group, to the task or to each other. With the increasing use of computers to support collaborative working, research is needed to investigate how cohesion develops and operates in computer-mediated groups.

## *Theoretical explanations*

Two different approaches have been used to explain CMC effects, one focusing on the reduced social context cues and the other on a change in social identity. In both, the concept of 'de-individuation' (the process of losing one's distinctiveness and sense of personal identity) is central. The principal difference is that the reduced social context cues approach proposes that email is de-individuating, compared to face-to-face interaction, while the social identity approach proposes that email can be de-individuating or individuating, depending on the context in which email is used.

Sproull and Kiesler (1991) propose that the reduced social context cues in CMC lead to less regard for other users and reduced audience awareness, and that this results in reduced inhibition in group members, leading to increased levels of self-disclosure and flaming. However, there are a number of major problems with this theory. Firstly, studies have shown differences in degree of flaming *across* different CMC conditions (e.g. Smolensky, Carmody and Halcomb, 1990), indicating that it cannot be the medium per se which is influencing communication behaviour. Moreover, even though this theory emphasises intrapersonal and interpersonal processes as mediating the effects of CMC, researchers have failed to collect user perceptions of each other and of the group. According to social identity theory, two important conditions influence de-individuation - the sense of group identity and the degree of personal identifiability to other group members. De-individuation is shown in those groups where the 'group' is emphasised more than the 'individual' and where levels of personal identifiability are low (Turner, Hogg, Oakes, Reicher and Wetherall, 1987). Social identity theory predicts that when individuals are de-individuated, adherence to group norms is high. Spears, Lea and Lee (1990) explain the normative and anti-normative effects of CMC using the social identity approach. However, although Spears *et al.* (1990) did find support for social identity theory (in the de-individuated conditions group members' attitudes moved in line with the group norms), they did not measure other factors involved in computer-mediated group interaction (for example group cohesion, flaming or self-disclosure).

There are a number of methodological problems with the research reported in this review. Specifically, most of the research was conducted in the laboratory, using artificial designs and procedures. For example, the size of discussion groups was small, discussion was often limited to a few minutes, frequently participants were unaccustomed to using email and tasks were very narrow. Therefore, it is not clear how much these results will generalise to group processes in real CMC systems.

## *Experimental rationale and hypotheses*

This study aims to address some of the criticisms of previous research raised in the review. A general criticism is that previous research has neglected to collect measures of the way users perceive each other and the group - this study will collect measures of interpersonal perception. Second, it is not clear that the results from the laboratory studies reviewed can be generalised to real CMC networks where larger numbers of people would be involved and discussion would take place over longer periods of time. This study is conducted in real working environments, therefore the effects of context, daily routine and workload that occur in normal everyday use of email are taken into account. In addition, in line with Huber's recommendations, the research will investigate whether social identity theory can explain computer-mediated group interaction effects.

In summary, this study will manipulate email conditions, which it is predicted will lead to different degrees of de-individuation, which in turn will lead to differential effects on group communication and interpersonal perception. The de-individuated group is predicted to be that which receives very little identifying information (i.e. Low Identifiability) and instructions emphasising the group (i.e. Group Salience). The following hypotheses will be tested:

1.  there will be less uninhibited communication (in terms of flaming and self-disclosure) in de-individuated groups;
2.  there will be more balanced group member participation (in terms of frequency of messages) in de-individuated groups;
3.  those participants in Low Identifiability conditions will perceive more group cohesion than those in High Identifiability conditions;
4.  those participants in Group Salience conditions will perceive more group cohesion than those in Individual Salience conditions.

## 11.2 Method

In total, 48 participants (37 males and 11 females) responded to a request posted on a number of different email networks within the UK. Participants were randomly assigned to groups of six with the constraint that each group contained at least one female participant. Participants were geographically dispersed and care was taken to ensure that volunteers from the same electronic network were not placed in the same groups. No one had previously met or spoken to another member of their group.

A 2 x 2 between subjects factorial design was employed, with Personal Identifiability (Low or High) and Group Salience (Individual or Group) as the independent variables. Two discussion groups were assigned to each condition. Personal Identifiability was manipulated by providing those in the High Identifiability condition with an electronic biographic database containing details of each group member. Participants in the Low Identifiability condition were given only the email usernames of other group members. Immersion in the group was manipulated by varying the emphasis of instructions given to participants. This has previously been shown to be sufficient to engender a sense of group membership (Turner *et al.*, 1987).

All participants were asked to complete a brief biographical questionnaire, containing items on education, employment, email use, hobbies and a personal description. After participants had been allocated to one of the groups, they were given instructions specific to the condition. This initiated the discussion period which lasted for two weeks. Each participant used their normal email terminal. Participants communicated by sending a message to the distribution list set up at the address for their group, which was then automatically distributed to other group members. Each group discussed the same topic. Participants were free to send as many messages as they wished, on as many days as they wished. At the end of the discussion period, participants completed a self-report questionnaire which contained measures of interpersonal perception.

## 11.3 Results

The analysis of the data will be considered in two sections - group communication and interpersonal perception.

### *Group communication*

The transcripts were coded blind by the researcher (i.e. all information that could be used to identify conditions or participants was removed). This coding noted the incidence of flaming and self-disclosure. Two types of flaming were differentiated - type A consisted of abusive or impolite comments directed towards participants while type B consisted of general comments containing uninhibited language. Self-disclosure was defined as any comments that revealed something private about the person. Tables 1, 2 and 3 show the total number of self-disclosure and flaming comments per condition. It can be seen that participants receiving a Low level of Identifiability produced very few examples of either kind of flaming. The observed frequencies were compared against expected values of equal distribution and they were not equally distributed for either type of flaming. Flaming therefore did not occur evenly across conditions and it can be seen that Identifiability was the significant factor in both types of flaming. Contrary to previous research it was the individuated, High Identifiability conditions that produced the most flaming not the impersonal, Low Identifiability conditions. Group Salience had little effect, with those in the Group and Individual conditions producing similar numbers of both types of flame.

The incidence of self-disclosure, illustrated in Table 3, indicates that the more that is known about other members of the group (i.e. High Identifiability groups), the more a person will disclose about themselves. Frequency of self-disclosure across conditions was significantly and strongly affected by the experimental manipulations. Participants were also asked if they felt more open to discussion of the topic using email, compared to face-to-face discussion. Those receiving High Identifiability reported feeling significantly more open to discussions than those receiving Low Identifiability, supporting the data in Table 3.

| | | **Identifiability** | | |
|---|---|---|---|---|
| | | Low | High | Totals |
| **Salience** | Individual | 1 | 13 | 14 |
| | Group | 4 | 8 | 12 |
| | Totals | 5 | 21 | 26 |

Chi=12.45; df=1; p<0.001

*Table 1. Frequency of Type A flaming.*

| | | **Identifiability** | | |
|---|---|---|---|---|
| | | Low | High | Totals |
| **Salience** | Individual | 4 | 13 | 17 |
| | Group | 2 | 11 | 13 |
| | Totals | 6 | 24 | 30 |

Chi=15.32; df=1; p<0.001

*Table 2. Frequency of Type B flaming.*

Table 4 shows the means and standard deviations for the number of messages sent per person in each condition over the two-week period. It can be seen that Identifiability has a strong and statistically significant effect on message-sending activity - participants receiving High Identifiability sent significantly more messages than those receiving Low Identifiability. The Group Salience manipulation had no significant effect, however there is a nearly significant interaction between Salience and Identifiability. This is probably due to the differences in message-sending activity between the Low and High conditions of groups receiving Individual Salience. When the standard deviations are examined it can be seen that there is more variability in the High Identifiability groups, while standard deviations are lower for the Low Identifiability groups indicating a more balanced distribution of messages sent by each group member.

In summary, it appears that Identifiability is a significant factor affecting uninhibited communication, where the more that is known about other members of the group then the more that people are prepared to flame and self-disclose. Limiting the amount of identifying information produces a more balanced discussion, although there was also less communication occurring in these groups.

## Inter-personal perception

Interpersonal perception was measured on seven-point Likert-type rating scale, where -3 indicated disagreement and +3 indicated agreement with a statement. As shown in Table 5, the Identifiability manipulation strongly and significantly affected perceptions of group cohesion, with more group cohesion occurring in the High Identifiability groups. The Group Salience manipulation was not significant. Both of these findings are contrary to predictions. Perceptions of other group members were generally favourable, as shown in Table 6. It can be seen that participants receiving Group Salience and High Identifiability liked other group members the most, although this interaction was not statistically significant.

| | **Identifiability** | | |
|---|---|---|---|
| | Low | High | Totals |
| Individual | 4 | 17 | 21 |
| Group | 1 | 31 | 32 |
| Totals | 5 | 48 | 53 |

Chi=42.62; df=1; p<0.001

*Table 3. Frequency of self-disclosure.*

In summary, the results showed that Identifiability rather than Group Salience was the important factor impacting on interpersonal perception. This is contrary to the predictions based on social identity theory that group cohesion would be highest in Group Salience and Low Identifiability groups.

## 11.4    Discussion

This study had two main purposes. The first was to consider the way that group members' perceptions of the group relate to group interaction and in particular to investigate whether social identity theory could be used to explain the effects of CMC. The second aim was to examine group interaction in *realistic* email discussion groups where the contexts had been manipulated to provide emphasis on a personal individual identity or an impersonal social identity.

The first conclusion to be drawn from the data presented here is that there is no support for the view that impersonal or 'de-individuated' contexts encourage uninhibited communication either in quantity or in quality. In fact the evidence here directly contradicts that found by Kiesler, Siegal and McGuire (1984). It was the conditions in which participants could be personally identified that produced higher levels of flaming and self-disclosure. Hence the rather 'technologically deterministic' arguments of Sproull and Kiesler (1991) regarding the effects of reduced social context cues are unfounded. More complex processes and factors are involved in influencing communication in electronic groups particularly as regards the extent to which people obey the social norms that govern communication and interaction in face-to-face contexts. Whatever leads to anti-normative behaviour in CMC systems, anonymity does not appear to be the critical factor.  If one takes the view that flaming and self-disclosure are more socio-emotional rather than task-based discussion, then the provision of personal information has encouraged and facilitated the groups to interact at that level. Whether this can be seen as a positive release of socio-emotional interaction or a negative release cannot be ascertained from this study - further research is needed.

Within this relatively realistic context, the prediction of more balanced participation in groups receiving limited identifying information was confirmed (Dubrovsky *et al.*, 1991), although there was also less communication occurring in these groups. The implications of this are important as regards the conclusions that can be drawn about the consequences of the use of CMC systems. It would appear that in circumstances where a high level of interactive discussion is desirable, this could be achieved by providing a means for the participants to obtain information about the other members of the group.  However, if equality of participation is the critical goal then the

| | | Identifiability | | | |
|---|---|---|---|---|---|
| | | Low | High | Means | |
| **Salience** | Individual | 3.2 (1.2) | 9.7 (5.3) | 6.45 | Identifiability F=10.05; df=1,44; p=0.002 Salience F=1.08; df=1,44; p=0.305 Interaction F=3.99; df=1,44; p=0.052 |
| | Group | 6.9 (4.9) | 8.4 (4.0) | 7.65 | |
| | Means | 5.05 | 9.05 | 7.05 | |

*Table 4. Mean number of messages sent in each condition (standard deviations in parentheses).*

anonymity of group members should be preserved. It is difficult to give guidelines on how to realise both high level of discussion and equal participation; further work needs to be conducted in this area.

The importance of believing oneself to be part of a group has been shown elsewhere to affect behaviour significantly (Tajfel, 1981). However, despite the vast literature in face-to-face group research, much of the previous CMC research has ignored group cohesion. Moreover, despite the implication of changes in interpersonal perception as a mediating influence in some theories of CMC (Sproull and Kiesler, 1991), measurements of interpersonal perception have not been collected. The study presented in this chapter produced an unexpected set of significant group cohesion

| | | Identifiability | | | |
|---|---|---|---|---|---|
| | | Low | High | Means | |
| **Salience** | Individual | -1.31 | 0.42 | -0.44 | Identifiability F=10.09; df=1,45; p=0.003 Salience F=0.56; df=1,45; p=0.460 Interaction F=0.76; df=1,45; p=0.387 |
| | Group | -0.73 | 0.36 | -0.18 | |
| | Means | -1.02 | 0.39 | -0.31 | |

*Table 5. Mean responses to the item: 'How cohesive was your group?'.*

| | **Identifiability** | | | |
|---|---|---|---|---|
| | | Low | High | Means |
| **Salience** | Individual | 0.15 | 0.42 | 0.29 |
| | Group | 0.36 | 1.20 | 0.78 |
| | Means | 0.26 | 0.81 | 0.54 |

Identifiability
F=2.60; df=1,42; p=0.115
Salience
F=1.80; df=1,42; p=0.187
Interaction
F=0.99; df=1,42; p=0.325

*Table 6. Mean responses to the item: 'Did you like the other participants?'*

findings, contrary to the predictions based on social identity theory. It was the manipulation of Personal Identifiability, not Group Salience, which significantly affected perceptions of group cohesion. Also contrary to social identity theory, the results showed that more group cohesion was perceived in groups receiving identifying information. However, it is not clear whether Identifiability directly affected these perceptions or whether they are affected by the increases in communication activity or uninhibited communication that occurred in these groups. It may be that group cohesion operates differently in computer-mediated groups and that the lack of non-verbal cues qualitatively affects interpersonal perception. The relationship between self-disclosure and group cohesion shown in previous face-to-face group research (Elias *et al.*, 1989) was shown in this study, yet it is not clear whether self-disclosure encouraged group cohesion or vice versa.

In conclusion, the research has contributed to an understanding of how the contexts of email affect group interaction, in particular where the levels of social identity of group members were investigated. Further research is needed to collect user perceptions of flaming to identify whether flaming is perceived as normative or anti-normative and standard measures need to be specified for flaming and self-disclosure. Further research is also needed into group cohesion. This is particularly important considering the group research which emphasises the important role that group cohesion plays in the performance and productivity of groups at work. Such results may have important implications for the implementation of Computer Supported Co-operative Work (CSCW) and CMC systems. Other aspects of the context such as task-type also need to be studied. Such work will contribute towards a culmination of results across contexts to help determine which features of CMC technology produce various outcomes and may also help clarify inconsistent results across studies. In the discussion of the findings from this study, it was suggested that some group processes may not operate in the same predictable ways in realistic computer-mediated groups as they do in face-to-face groups. In their paper, '*Groups are not always the same*', Lyytinen, Maaranen and Knuuttila (1994) come to a similar conclusion when they propose that CMC research so far has been technology-focused and they suggest that new, computer-mediated, group processes need to be investigated. In the words of Sproull and Kiesler (1991), 'electronic groups are not just traditional groups whose members use a computer'.

# 12. Interactional implications of computer mediation in emergency calls

## Luís Pérez-González

## 12.1 Introduction

This chapter reports the findings of a corpus-based study of electronic mediation in calls from members of the public for emergency assistance in the United Kingdom. From a study of 66 conversational samples, it is argued that electronic mediation affects the unfolding of the interaction between the participants in a number of ways. Our analysis draws upon Halliday's (1978) stratified view of language and accounts for the influence of electronic mediation in terms of specific field, tenor and mode constraints on the ongoing conversation.

The chapter begins with an ethnographic characterisation of the institutional setting under scrutiny, in order to spell out the computer-mediated nature of our data. After describing the construction of our corpus and restricting the scope of our analysis to a specific stage of emergency calls, we embark on the analysis of our data. The conversational effects of electronic mediation are examined in relation to three major variables. First, the institutionally relevant agenda (field constraints); second, the participants' acquaintance with the demands of the medium (mode constraints); finally, the relationship which emerges between the interactants (tenor constraints). The concluding section explores the relevance of CMC studies to the enhancement of interaction in emergency calls by considering some specific applications.

## 12.2 Emergency calls as computer-mediated interaction

### An ethnographic characterisation of calls for emergency assistance

The phone-mediated interaction between members of the public and emergency organisations has become an increasingly frequent type of social encounter over the last three decades. Citizens (C) dialling the emergency number aim to secure the mobilisation of the institution's remedial resources, while their organisational co-interactants are expected to assess the nature and the urgency of the incident reported before agreeing or refusing to mobilise. The incumbents of the institutional rôle in these conversational events are, successively, the operator, the call-taker and the dispatcher of assistance. Operators implement a call-screening policy, elicit a number of basic data and connect C to the relevant emergency service, such as the fire brigade, ambulance service or police. Call-takers (CT) interact with C, probe for detailed information about the incident, process the ensuing data in institutionally relevant terms and decide on the type and priority of the assistance to be dispatched. For their part, dispatchers are in charge of selecting specific units for the implementation of the remedial action. In the remainder of this chapter, we will restrict our account to the analysis of conversational interaction between C and CT.

Some of the most recent studies on emergency interaction (Zimmerman, 1992a; Whalen, 1994) have focused on the constant transformations which are taking place in this professional setting with regard to the professional practices of the console and switchboard officers. As we will discuss later in this chapter, the upshot of these changes is that the interaction between C and CT is becoming increasingly constrained by the use of certain technological devices, in particular computer-aided electronic data-forms. In broad terms, CT's job nowadays involves the translation of C's demands into codes or other institutionally recognisable electronic inputs. Given that this categorisation-task is to be completed in full before CT's report can be transmitted electronically to the dispatcher, it is reasonable to conclude that computer mediation has an important bearing on the process whereby emergency calls are managed.

## The data - a corpus of computer-mediated emergency calls

This paper will revolve around a corpus of 66 calls to the switchboards of a number of British fire brigades, ambulance dispatch-centres and police-stations. For reasons which fall beyond the scope of this paper (Pérez-González, 1999), our corpus was divided into three different sections depending on the nature of the incident at issue:

- Section A includes calls seeking the dispatch of fire brigade or ambulance units, made on the premises of incidents which are currently in progress;
- Section B consists of a number of citizens' reports, complaints and help-requests to the police. These concern not only current emergencies, but also other incidents which C regards as a potential safety hazard;
- Section C includes personal and bomb-threats.

The examples included in this paper are all excerpts from our corpus samples. The recordings were kindly provided by J.P. French Associates, a York-based consultancy which had previously used this material in the course of their speaker-profiling work as expert witnesses in the field of forensic linguistics. The recordings were carefully transcribed, paying particular attention to the keyboard sounds - which constitute the interface between the computer-aided form and the actual speech - as well as the emergence of the latter at specific stages of the interaction between the participants. In this connection, the structural organisation of emergency calls should be briefly dealt with before proceeding with our characterisation of this discourse-type as computer-mediated communication.

The scrutiny of our corpus samples revealed the existence of a *canonical structural patterning* which would seem to hold across individual encounters, thus corroborating previous research on this issue (Eglin and Wideman, 1986; Whalen and Zimmerman, 1987). Emergency 999 calls exhibit, within a range of orderly variation, a distinctive organisation of sequences which we will now enumerate in point form (see also Figure 1):

- First, an *opening sequence*, revolving mainly around CT's categorical self-identification and oriented to confirm that C has reached the interlocutor required
- Second, C's *request for organisational assistance*. This is the first and only interactional space for C to deliver his/her report of the incident without CT's mediation
- Third, the *interrogative series* (IS), where CT probes for information on the nature and urgency of the assistance required. It is worth emphasising that the exchange of questions/answers at this stage takes place while the response to C's request is still pending
- Fourth, the *organisational response* to C's request for assistance. From an organisational standpoint, the granting/denial of assistance indicates that the interactional business has been concluded
- Finally, the *closing sequence*.

## The interrogative series as a computer-mediated segment

Unlike other constitutive elements of emergency calls, the structure and length of the

---

**The canonical organisation of an emergency call from an ethnomethodological standpoint** (Sample A.12/001-029/abridged)

| Opening Section | CT:<br>C: | Hello, fire brigade?<br>Yes, | categorical identification<br>acknowledgement |
|---|---|---|---|
| Request | | I've got a fire at twenty-seven, Wake Green road. | request |
| Interrogative Section | CT:<br>C:<br>CT:<br>C:<br>CT:<br>C:<br><br><br>CT:<br><br>C:<br>CT: | What is on fire?<br>The carpet...<br>And which town or village is this in?<br>Sorry?<br>Which town or village?<br>it's Sheffield, it's Wake Green road, number twenty-seven Wake Green road, near Cape Hill road.<br>Right; and the carpet is inside the property, is it?<br>Yes it is.<br>Right | question 1<br>answer 1<br>question 2<br>repair<br>repeat question 2<br>answer 2<br><br><br>acknowledgement + question 3<br>answer 3<br>acknowledgement |
| Response | <br>C: | Fire Brigade is on its way.<br>Lovely, | grant of assistance<br>acknowledgement |
| Closing | <br>CT:<br><br>C: | thank you!<br>Thank you. Bye!<br><br>Bye! | ack.+ pre-closing item 1<br>pre-closing item 2 + terminal item 1.<br>terminal item 2. |

*Figure 1.*

interrogative series are highly variable across individual encounters. The final shape of this 'complaint-remedy bracket' (Zimmerman, 1984) depends mainly on CT's discretion as to which of C's contributions are acceptable both from a quantitative and a qualitative point of view. The analysis of our data suggests that CT's discretion is, in its turn, highly contingent on the computer's mediation while processing the information elicited from C.

As the reader will have inferred, emergency calls constitute an idiosyncratic instance of CMC, insofar as only one of the participants (CT) is aware of such constraints on the ongoing interaction. This fact is particularly relevant to the study of structural variation in the interrogative series, which is built upon the negotiation between one conversant who is acquainted with the relevant organisational procedures of interaction and another one who is not expected to be familiar with such specialised technical conventions (Drew 1991). CT's management of a given call draws upon certain institutional resources whose relevance has been checked out in the course of a long chain of prior institutional encounters and have subsequently joined the organisation's 'social stock of knowledge' (Linell and Luckman, 1991). For their part, C approaches the event with the same expectations as for any other phone-mediated type of service encounter. This being so, an 'interactional asynchrony' (Whalen, Zimmerman and Whalen 1988) underlies the unfolding of the interrogative series. On the one hand, C makes use of their mundane interactional skills, which are idiosyncratic and result in an individualised report of the incident. On the other hand, the institutional constraints on CT's talk often result in an impersonal, efficiency-seeking management of the request for assistance. In sum, a substantial amount of interactional tolerance is required from both participants. While C's emotional strain may lead him or her to ignore CT's directions on *what* to report and *how* to do it, CT's impersonal demeanour may obscure the bearing of the interrogation on the organisational decision (not) to mobilise. The ensuing situation has been described by Ventola (1989) as follows:

> When an interactant gets involved in a co-operative situation, he or she may start with a certain planned generic structure in mind. But, once involved in an interaction, the negotiation with the fellow participant on how to proceed begins, and the planned unfolding of the interaction may change. Interaction is built by matching interactants' expectations and goals.
>
> (Ventola, 1989, p. 136)

Our corpus shows that the interrogative series is the structural constituent of emergency calls which best illustrates the effects of computer mediation in this professional setting. Consequently, the discussion in the remainder of this chapter will concentrate on the computer-mediated interaction which takes place between C and CT within the interrogative series.

## 12.3 Register-related aspects of CMC

Regardless of the methodological differences between individual approaches, work currently being undertaken on service encounters and institutional interaction has

demonstrated the influence of *context* on the organisation and unfolding of conversational events (Ventola, 1987; Zimmerman and Boden, 1991; Drew and Heritage, 1992). For purposes of presentation, this section will adopt Halliday's (1978) widely accepted stratified view of language. His systemic approach regards conversational phenomena - *language* - as the realisation of specific contextual constraints or *register*. More specifically, our characterisation of emergency calls as CMC will consider the three register variables in turn - *field* (what is going on in the interaction), *mode* (what rôle the communication channel plays in the encounter) and finally, *tenor* (the relationship between the participants). Particular attention will be paid to the mode-related constraints, as they play an important rôle in the configuration of emergency calls as a type of CMC.

### Field-related constraints and CMC

CT's interactional performance in emergency calls is oriented to the assembly of the Dispatch Package (DP) (Zimmerman, 1992b). This should ideally contain any item of information that may contribute to maximise the efficiency of the dispatch process. Although the institutional guidelines to be followed by CT when processing incoming calls vary across corpus sections and, thereby, depend on the incident-type at issue, there are a number of tasks involved in the assembly of DP which remain constant:

First of all, it is crucial to determine the precise nature, urgency and scope of the incident reported:

(Note: underlining indicates emphasis)

```
Example 1    Sample B.4 (038-066; abridged)
038    CT:   en'what's the problem?
039     C:   (0.5)
040          (there's > somebuddy (.) actin'suspiciousl- <) =
             hullo?
041    CT:   yeah. = 'm still here. =
042     C:   = > there's somebuddy actin' suspiciously. < (.)
             uhm- I'think it's                    aston
043          roa:d. (...)
060    CT:   = right'en w- how're they acting suspiciously?
061     C:   it's not like- I don't know, they were very close
             t'the windows like (.)
062          (trying to  bang the windows)
063          (3.5)
064          (I came'round the back. = I went j'st like) (    )
065          (1.0)
066          (knock'em round (    ) somebuddy (    ) 'f somebuddy
             else.)
```

Second, CT's probes for information should yield a highly precise location of the ongoing incident:

**Example 2**   Sample B.3 (041–055)
```
041           mister murphy where'r'ju calling from? =
042    C:     = (     -) I'm callin from a phone box onne corner.
043    CT:    right. (.) avershore... what district's that / aston
              is it?
044    C:     pard'n?
045    CT:    whad'district is th't?
046    C:     (0.5)
047           my address?
048    CT:    no. (.) what district's that you're innat the moment
              h?
049    C:      avershore.
050    CT:    yeah th- that's the aston area?
051    C:     pardon?
052    CT:    is that the aston area?
053    C:     e::h (.) ( I think it iz) in oldham area.
054    CT:    oldham area.
055    C:     yeah.
```

The management of calls reporting incidents which involve actual or potential emergencies should shed light on issues such as 'descriptions of suspects, whether they are armed, whether they are still present at the scene or the direction and means of their flight' (Zimmerman, 1992b, p. 422):

**Example 3**   Sample B.8 (013–021)
```
013    CT:    what does she looks like?
014           (0.1)
015           what's she wearin'?
016    C:     turquoise blue jacket,
017    CT:    (0.5)
018           turquoise   blue je:ans]
019    C:           blue jea:ns]
020    CT:    .h how old is she?
021    C:     nineteen twenny.
```

Zimmerman (1992b, p. 423) offers the following illustration of a DP from his corpus:

```
23:03         2270 5 Av. N.          pergun p1
Ø             comp says people are shooting guns at that address —
              no one shot yet. Says they will shoot cops. Then
              hung up
```

The first line in this DP indicates the address of the emergency and the time at which the latter was reported. It also represents two of the hundreds of codes used in some dispatch-centres, which CT 'must memorize and enter without error as the system will accept only the correct code or abbreviation' (Zimmerman,1992b, p. 423). In this case 'pergun' stands for 'person with a gun', whereas 'p1' equates with 'priority 1'.

## Mode-related constraints and CMC

It becomes evident from the foregoing discussion that the task of DP-assembly involves the use of *coding conventions* which enable the electronic processing of the incoming information and the transmission of the latter to the dispatcher. Accordingly, the field constraints on emergency interaction are inextricably related to their mode-related counterparts. In other words, what *goes on* in the conversational encounter is contingent on the fact that emergency interaction is a form of CMC. As our corpus data confirm, in most dispatch-consoles a call-taker receives the phone call and, while engaged in interaction with the caller, enters information into a form onto the computer screen, assembling a textual record - in effect, a documentary representation - of the reported trouble or event. This form is then electronically transmitted to another communications centre staff member serving the rôle of dispatcher. (Whalen, 1994, p. 4)

This being so, the assembly of DP is mediated by the task of filling the relevant computer-aided dispatch (CAD) data-form. It should be noted that DP and CAD determine both the choice and the order of CT's questions. It is precisely on this insight that our characterisation of the interrogative series as a computer-mediated stretch of discourse is premised. There are number of distinctive features of CAD that are worth looking at:

- the completion of the CAD data-form takes place in real interactional time and is simultaneous with CT's monitoring of C's contributions. Therefore, CT may find it occasionally difficult to keep up with the pace of the interaction while fulfilling their institutional duties;
- the CAD-mediated assembly of DP is the process whereby a call for assistance is represented in institutionally relevant terms and, thereby, warrants some sort of organisational response;
- the CAD data-form is intended to help CT with the managing of the call. More specifically, it aims to minimise the differences between CT's behaviour across individual calls. In some cases, however, the *standardisation* of the management-strategies and the *routinisation* of the recording practices clash with other institutional aims, such as CT's duty to provide C with 'recipient-designed answers' (Sacks, 1992). Should CT's behaviour abide mainly by the first two goals, emotionally strained Cs may feel that their request for assistance is not being managed with a sufficiently individualised concern by CT.

The recordings and transcripts of our corpus samples attest to the mediation of CAD data-forms in emergency interaction, as shown in Example 4 below:

```
Example 4    Sample A.30 (002-018)
002     O:    (it's) coventry 3. 6. 3. d'ble two:   9.
003     CT:   3. 6. 3. 2. 2. 9.
004           [kb————————
005     O:    go'head.
006           ——]
007     CT:   hello. fire brigade?
008     C:    hm- I'd like tuh repo:rt a fire plea:se.
009     CT:   yes?
010C=   h)    it's th'smoke pourin'outuv (h) (.) 1 (.) 4. 6 en 1.
              4. 8              norrthmarine   road
011           [kb————————
012     CT:   (2.0)
013           ————
014           1. 4. 6 en 1. 4. 8 northmarine road.
015           ——————————————————————————--
016     C:    yeah.   they're holiday flats I b'lie:ve.
017           ——————————--]
018     CT:   oh  right.
```

The CAD-filling activity is audible on the recordings in the form of keyboard sounds, which are represented in the transcripts with the symbol <kb> followed by a series of dashes whose number depends on the duration of the sounds. The transcript layout makes it clear that keyboard sounds start as C is probed for DP-relevant information such as C's identity, location and other ancillary detail and that keyboard action lags behind the items of information which are being recorded.

## Tenor-related aspects in CMC

The tenor variables determine the interactional relationship which participants engage in through conversation. Given that field, mode and tenor constraints mutually determine one another, the conversational interaction between C and CT will display the consequences of computer mediation as outlined above. In what follows we will discuss those conversational phenomena which best illustrate the underlying influence of DP and CAD data-forms.

As was suggested above, 'the moment-by-moment, turn-by-turn unfolding of the vocal exchange between the call-taker and citizen caller and the concurrent actions by the call-taker at the keyboard in the CAD' are two simultaneous processes (Whalen, 1994, p. 8). As a result, CT faces a difficult dilemma as they strive both to complete the electronic data-form efficiently and to show their sensitivity to C's emotional strain. Our corpus samples suggest that CT makes use of certain processing practices which constitute a distinctive feature of emergency interaction and may be outlined in the following terms. Once CT has obtained enough information on one of the DP-constitutive issues, they take the interactional floor back from C. CT then puts another question which is topically focused on the next relevant DP-issue, while typing the information C has just delivered. Given the lack of pauses during which to carry out this typing-task, CT has to find other alternative ways to keep up with the interactional pace of the encounter. CT deals with this timing problem by making use of repetition-shaped turn holders, which help their typing not to lose track of the ongoing interaction, as shown in Example 5:

```
Example 5   Sample A.13 (014-032)
014    CT:   ((coughs)) 'n what's on fire?
             ———————]
016     C:   (1.0)
             [kb———-
             wel'l, (.) it's the kitchen I'thi:nk.
             ————————————————————-]
020    CT:   the kitchen,
021     C:   (0.5)
             [kb———
             yea:h.
             ————-]
025    CT:   .h izit jer house?
             [kb————————
027     C:   (1.0)
             ————
             no. it's the next door  neighbour's!
             ———————————————————————-]
031    CT:    it's jer next door neighbour. (.) .h so that's
             thirty four handsworth grove
             day:esmore.
```

The most immediate implication of the CAD-system's influence on the assembly of DP is that CT is often required to abide by the geography of the electronic data form, such that certain issues have to be necessarily elicited before others. In this connection, let us consider Whalen's (1994, p. 5) sample of a typical CAD data-form in Figure 2.

The CAD form displayed above has a bearing on the ordering of CT's probes for information, as no less than five of the slots must be compulsorily filled before the emergency-report can be electronically transmitted to the actual dispatcher of assistance. These codes are represented in bold characters and correspond to the nature of the emergency (INC), its location (LOC), the priority granted to the request of help (PR), the phone number at the location (PHO) and, finally, the internal extension number of the incumbent CT (SRC). According to our corpus, the *compartmentalised layout* of the CAD sheets is to be held responsible for the lack of interactional flexibility which CT sometimes exhibits when interacting with an emotionally strained C.

The electronic mediation in the negotiation between C and CT is not restricted to the order of the questions, but extends also to the constraints governing the processing of the incoming information. The data provided by C have to be coded according to

```
INC: _____  _____  TY:_____ FD/CTY: _____ /
_____ ID: _____
LOC: _____  EUG PR: _____  TY/NM:
_____
PHO: _____  X: _____  PH ADR: _____
_____ FL: _____
SRC: _____ XST: _____  MAP:
_____ DIST: _____
BREATH: ____ CONSC: ___ AGE: ____ SEX: _____ AGYS: ____ ___
___ ___ INI: ____
CALLER: _____  CONT: _____
REF: _____
ADR: _____  EUG   DISP:
_____ CSN: _____
DTL:
_____
_____
```

*Figure 2. Sample of an electronic data-form in a CAD-system.*

the institutionally relevant conventions; in other words, CT's duty is to represent the incident in organisationally acceptable codes. Consequently, CT's need to accommodate C's responses within a single slot — and, thereby, to choose each code with maximum precision — has interactonal consequences.

As was mentioned above, the nature of the current incident is one of the pieces of information relevant to the DP. This being so, CT's attempt to obtain a reliable categorisation of the emergency and to secure a precise account of the incident from C will often require additional of clarificatory questions:

```
Example 6    Sample B.8 (005-012)
005     C:   = hello. = there's a youn'girl't (.) marine centre
             widda flick knife.
006          (1.0)
007          she's following old people'round for money.
008     CT:  (1.0)
009          she's following'em around'r asking'em for money? =
010     C:   = no = she's  followi::n them.
011          (1.0)
012          she asked me but I said no::.

Example 7    Sample B.26 (005-016; abridged)
005     C:   yeah. (.) drugs're bein' passed through di chain.
```

```
006   CT:   through  di:?
007    C:   CHAIN!
008   CT:   chain's PUB?
009    C:   yeah.
015         > en how d'ju know this h? <
016    C:   becuz I've j'st bought some.
```

**Example 8**   Sample C.3 (008-013)
```
008         .h an'incendjary device cud be placed en will be
009         placed between now and the la:s' train tonight. (.)
            .h so I ('ll) suggest that
010         yuh remember dis whadwe'v sed, .h en you get hold of
            people off the
011         station (.) so that's all I'm gonna say just //
            once].
012   CT:   okay. // 'en = areju givimme any code?
013    C:   ((puts the phone down))
```

Another interactional issue which is subject to electronic mediation is the elicitation and processing of the location of the incident, as 'locations must be entered as either an exact address; a street 'hundred block'; a landmark (preceded by a landmark designator...') that the CAD system recognizes and will then replace, as the form is transmitted to the dispatcher, with the landmark's official address; or an intersection' (Whalen, 1994, p. 26). Our corpus illustrates this point with multiple examples of locational formulations which must be re-elaborated so that CT is able to enter them in the CAD system, as in Example 9 below:

**Example 9**   Sample A.17 (002-012)
```
002   CT:   fire service what's di  address?
003    C:   it's flat o:ne h,
004   CT:   flat one,
005    C:   .h hundred'n te:n h,
006   CT:   a hundred'n te:n,
007    C:   summerfield roa:d,
008   CT:   hundred'n ten summerfield road,
009    C:   wolly range h h.
010   CT:   (0.5)
011         en where'bouts in summerfield road is it?
012    C:   it's halfway do- it's off withington road.
```

There are also examples of CT's preference for map-based formulations of location rather than compass-based ones:

**Example 10** Sample A.9 (008–012)
```
008     C:   hello. > uh my n- my n- in my neighbours' garden
             there's a large fire eh-
009          a shed burning extremely vigorously eh very close to
             their house. < (.) has
010          dis been reported // to ju?]
011     CT:  .h yes it has h.]  > cudju j'st confirm th'address
             h for me plea:se? <
012     C:   the address is one five two billesley roa:d.
```

Finally, the interactional relationship which holds between C and CT is determined by the nature of the emergency at issue. Issues such as the description of suspects or the means of their flight, to give just two examples, do not have to be elucidated in canonical calls to the fire brigade, although they are usually crucial for the assembly of DP in calls to the police. In other words, not all the slots displayed in the CAD data-form are to be necessarily filled in all cases. More specifically, typing certain codes at the INC slot would seem to render some of the remaining slots idle, thus waiving the need for CT to probe for certain elements of information.

Our corpus demonstrates that the interrogative series in section B calls is the most complex as regards the number of institutional requirements to be met and the amount of ancillary information to be provided by C. The source of the problem, the presence of guns or knifes, the number of suspects, descriptions or time-lapse between the occurrence of the incident and the time of the call are some well-documented constituents of DP in section B calls. As far as section A and C calls are concerned, it is noteworthy that the location of the troublesome incident deserves maximum attention, while the account of C's reasons for the categorisation of the incident as a current or impending emergency is often dispensed with by CT.

Pérez-González (1999) attests the existence of important differences in the length of the interrogative series across incident-types. A number of reasons are proposed to account for this trend. Although space restrictions preclude discussing this aspect in detail, let us note that, in sections A and C, the callers are aware of the imminence of the reported event. Accordingly, they feel empowered to challenge some of CT's directions and, in some cases, to impose a specific line of action on the institutional interactant. For their part, callers participating in section B encounters have to *argue for*, rather than simply *report*, the problematic nature of a given event. This correlates with a more submissive interactional status on the part of C, such that the ensuing interaction abides by the canonical expectations which govern the unfolding of conversation in institutional settings.

## 12.4 Conclusion: the social relevance of CMC studies
In this chapter we have characterised the interrogative series in emergency calls for assistance as a CMC-event. In recent years, certain electronic systems of information-processing have been introduced in this institutional setting in order to standardise the work of the institutional interactants and, hence, to maximise the efficiency and

optimise the resources of the emergency services. This electronic mediation has proved to have consequences for:

- the restriction in the range of issues to be dealt with during the conversational event;
- the rôle played by the electronic tools available to the professional interactant;
- the conversational relationship which holds between the participants.

In this concluding section we would like to draw the reader's attention to the immediate social relevance of these CMC-related insights. Interestingly enough, the analysis of CMC itself may seem to warn us against the dangers involved in the use of electronic devices such as CAD-systems. The analysis would suggest that electronic data-entry forms need to be refined and their compartmentalised layout scrapped in favour of a more flexible arrangement which would allow CT to navigate freely through the slots while interacting with C. The fact that CT is *electronically forced* to type in certain codes before they can probe for other interactional issues often minimises their room for interactional manoeuvring. Their insistence on obtaining C's response to the current slot may lead the latter to challenge CT's probes for information. Emotionally strained callers often fail to see the relevance of certain questions, mainly those they had not anticipated before making the call, to the securing of an organisational response. This being so, their challenges to CT's requirements may trigger off an interactional dispute whose consequences may be fatal in some cases (Whalen, Zimmerman and Whalen, 1988; Pérez-González, 1999).

The static or synoptic character of currently available CAD-systems, however, has been exploited by researchers interested in other conversational phenomena taking place within the domain of emergency interaction. Hoax calls to the emergency services have proliferated in the last few years and constitute an onerous drain on the organisations' logistical and economical resources. In this connection, Pérez-González (1999) has attempted to demonstrate the feasibility of detecting hoax calls, on the grounds that malicious encounters tend to deviate from the institutionally favoured path of interaction. Computer mediation has been found responsible for the activation of certain register constraints which remain invariable, to a large extent, across individual encounters. Although further work is still required in this area, it is now a well-documented fact that computer-mediated interaction determines CT's perceptual categorisation of C's performance in a given encounter as either typical, i.e. genuine, or deviant, i.e. malicious, with respect to the generic conventions of this professional setting. These particular applications aside, we hope to have demonstrated the social relevance of CMC studies, a growing field of scholarship within the broader domain of applied linguistics, to the enhancement of human communication in institutional settings.

# Bibliography

Adrianson, L., and Hjelmquist, E. (1991). Group processes in face-to-face and computer-mediated communication. *Behaviour and Information Technology*, 10:4, 281-296.

Akmajian A., R.A. Demers, A.K. Farmer and R.M. Harnish. (1995). *Linguistics: An Introduction to Language and Communication*. 4th Edition. Cambridge, Mass.: MIT Press.

Angell, D. and B. Heslop. (1994). *The Elements of E-Mail Style: Communicate Effectively via Electronic Mail*. Reading, Mass.: Addison-Wesley.

Angiolillo, J.S., H.E. Blanchard, E.W. Israelski and A. Mané. (1997). Technology constraints of video-mediated communication. In Finn, K.E., Sellen, A.J. and Wilbur, S.B. (eds), *Video-mediated Communication*, pp. 51-73. New Jersey: Lawrence Erlbaum Associates.

Aronoff, M. (1994). Spelling as Culture. In W. C. Watt (ed.), *Writing Systems and Cognition: Perspectives from Psychology, Physiology, Linguistics, and Semiotics*, pp. 67-86. Dordrecht: Kluwer Academic Publishers.

Ausubel, D. P. (1968). *Educational Psychology*. New York: Holt, Rinehart and Winston.

Berkenkotter, M. and T. Huckin. (1995). *Genre Knowledge in Disciplinary Communication. Cognition/ Culture/ Power* . Hillsdale, N.J.: Lawrence Erlbaum.

Blakemore, D. (1992). *Understanding Utterances*. Oxford: Blackwell.

Boden, D. (1990). The world as it happens: Ethnomethodology and Conversation Analysis. In Ritzer, G. (ed), *Frontiers of Social Theory*, pp. 185-213. New York: Columbia University Press.

Bowers, J., J. Pycock, J. and J. O'Brien. (1996). Talk and embodiment in collaborative virtual environments. In *CHI'96 Electronic proceedings*, http://www.acm.org/sigchi/chi96/proceedings/papers/Bowers/jb_txt.ht.

Bowers, J. and J. Churcher. (1988). Local and global structuring of computer-mediated-communication: Developing linguistic perspectives on CSCW in COSMOS in CSCW 88. *Proceedings of the conference on Computer-supported cooperative work*, pp. 125- 139. Portland: ACM.

Britton, K. and A.C. Graesser (eds). (1996). *Models of Understanding Text* . Hillsdale, NJ: Lawrence Erlbaum Associates.

Brown, P. and S.C. Levinson. (1978). *Politeness: Some universals in language usage*. 1987 reissue. Cambridge: Cambridge University Press.

Burks, A. (1949). Icon, Index and Symbol. In *Philosophical and Phenomenological Research* IX/4, June 1949, pp. 673-689.

Buxton, W.A.S. (1997). Living in augmented reality: ubiquitous media and reactive environments. In Finn, K.E., Sellen, A.J. and Wilbur, S.B. (eds). *Video-mediated Communication*. Hillsdale, N.J.: Lawrence Erlbaum Associates, 1997.

Cathcart, R. S. and L.A. Samovar. (1992). *Small Group Communication*. Dubuque, IA: WCB Publishers.

Chafe, W. and J. Danielewicz. (1987). Properties of Spoken and Written Language. In Horowitz, R., Samuels, J. (eds). *Comprehending Oral and Written Language*, pp. 83-113. San Diego: Academic Press.

Charney, D. (1994). The Effect of Hypertext on Processes of Reading and Writing. In C. L. Selfe and S. Hilligoss (eds). *Literacy and Computers: The Complications of Teaching and Learning with Technology*. New York: The Modern Language Association of America.

Cho, N. (1996). Linguistic Features of Electronic Mail: Results from a Pilot Study. Paper presented at the Australian and New Zealand Communication Association Annual Conference, Brisbane, July 1996.

Conklin J. (1987). Hypertext: An Introduction and Survey. In *IEEE Computer*, 20/9, pp. 17-41.

Cononelos, T. and M. Oliva. (1993). Using Computer-Networks to Enhance Foreign-Language Culture Education. In *Foreign Language Annals*, 26/4, pp. 527-534.

Coulmas, F. (1989). *The Writing Systems of the World*. Oxford: Blackwell.

Coupland, N., K. Grainger and J. Coupland. (1988). Politeness in context: Intergenerational issues (Review article)'. In *Language in Society*, 17/2, pp. 253-262.

Davies, F. and Greene, T. (1984). *Reading for Learning in the Sciences*. Edinburgh: Oliver and Boyd.

Dillon A., C. McKnight and J. Richardson. (1993). Space - The Final Chapter or Why Physical Representations are not Semantic Intentions. In Dillon A., C. McKnight and J. Richardson (eds), *Hypertext: a psychological perspective*. Chichester: Ellis Horwood.

Drew, P. and J. Heritage. (1992). Analysing talk at work: an introduction. In Drew, P. and J. Heritage (eds.) *Talk at Work: Interaction in Institutional Settings*, pp. 3-65. Cambridge: Cambridge University Press.

Drew, P. (1991). Asymmetries of knowledge in conversational interaction. In Marková, I. and K. Foppa (eds.). *Asymmetries of Dialogue*, pp. 21-48. Hemel Hempstead: Harvester Wheatsheaf.

DuBartell, D. (1995). Discourse Features of Computer-Mediated Communication: 'Spoken like' and 'Written like'. In B.Warvik, S.-K. Tanskanen and R. Hiltunen (eds), *Organization in Discourse*. Proceedings from the Turku Conference, pp. 231-241. Turku: University of Turku.

Dubrovsky, V., Kiesler, S. and Sethna, B. N. (1991). The equalisation phenomenon. *Human-Computer Interaction*, 6, pp. 119-146.

Dunning T. (1993). Accurate methods for the statistics of surprise and coincidence. *Computational Linguistics*, 19:1, pp. 61-74.

Eglin, P. and D. Wideman (1986). Inequality in professional service encounters: verbal strategies of control versus task performance in calls to the police. *Zeitschrift für Soziologie*, 15:5, pp. 341-362.

Eklundh, K. S. (1986). Dialogue Processes in Computer Mediated Communication. Linkoping: Linkoping Studies in Arts and Science, 6.

Elias, F. G., Johnson, M. E. and J.B. Fortman. (1989). Task-focused self-disclosure. *Small Group Behaviour*, 20:1, pp. 87-96.

Ferrara, K., Brunner, H. and G. Whittemore. (1991). Interactive Written Discourse as an Emergent Register. Written Communication, 8:1, pp. 8-35.

Finholt, T., Sproull, L. and Kiesler, S. (1990). Communication and performance in ad hoc task groups. In J. Galegher, R. Kraut, and C. Egido (eds.), *Intellectual Teamwork*, pp. 291-325. Hillsdale, NJ: Erlbaum.

Flood, J. (ed) (1989). *Understanding Reading Comprehension: Cognition, Language and the Structure of Prose* . Newark, De: International Reading Association.

Gardner, R.C. (1985). *Social Psychology and Second Language Learning: the Rôle of Attitudes and Motivation*. London: Edward Arnold.

Garrett, P., Giles, H. and Coupland, N. (1989). The Contexts of Language Learning - Extending the intergroup model of second language acquisition. In S. Ting-Toomey and P. Causeney (eds.) *Language Communication and Culture: Current Directions* . Annual of International and Intercultural Communication, Vol. 13, pp. 201-221. Newbury Park, Calif: Sage.

George, F.H. (1973). *The Brain as a Computer*. 2nd Edition. Oxford: Pergamon Press.

Graham, M. B. and David C. (1996). Power and Politeness: Administrative Writing in an "Organized Anarchy". *Journal of Business and Technical Communication*, 10:1, pp. 5-27.

Gruber, H. (1996a). Themenentwicklung in wissenschaftlichen e-mail Diskussionslisten. Ein Vergleich zwischen einer moderierten und einer nichtmoderierten Liste. In R. Weingarten (ed) *Sprachwandel durch den Computer*, pp. 105-131. Opladen: Westdeutscher Verlag.

Gruber, H. (1996b). Aspects of power and communication in scholarly e-mail discussion lists. Excluding practices and peer-group formation. Paper presented at the 1st Knowledge and Discourse Conference, Hongkong, June 1996.

Hagge, J. and C. Kostelnick. (1989). Linguistic Politeness in Professional Prose: A Discourse Analysis of Auditors' Suggestion Letters, with Implications for Business and Communication Pedagogy. *Written Communication*, 6, pp. 312-39.

Halliday, M. A. K. (1978). *Language as Social Semiotic: The Social Interpretation of Language and Meaning*. London: Edward Arnold.

Herring, S. C. (1994). Politeness in computer culture: Why women thank and men flame. In Bucholtz, M., Liang, A. C., Sutton, L. and Hines, C. (eds.) *Cultural Performances: Proceedings of the Third Berkeley Women and Language Conference*. Berkeley: Berkeley Women and Language Group, pp. 278-294.

Huber, G. P. (1990). A theory of the effects of advanced IT on organizational design, intelligence and decision-making. *Academy of Management Review*. 15:1, pp. 47-71.

Ikeda, K.A. (1996). Social Psychological Approach to Networked Reality. *IEICE Transactions on Information and Systems*, E77D(12), pp. 1390-1396.

Jones, S. (1995). Understanding community in the information age. In S. Jones (ed.), *Cybersociety Computer-mediated Communication and Community*, pp. 11-35. Thousand Oak: Sage.

Katz S. M. (1996). Distribution of context words and phrases in text and language modelling. *Natural Language Engineering*. 2:1, pp. 15-59.

Kiesler, S. and Sproull, L. (1986). Response effects in the electronic survey. *Public Opinion Quarterly*, 50, pp. 402-413.

Kiesler, S., Siegal, J. and T. W. McGuire. (1984). Social psychological aspects of CMC. *American Psychologist*. 39:10, pp. 1123-1134.

Kim, C. (1990). *Hangul ui yoksa wa mirae [The History and Future of Hangul]*. Seoul: Yolhwadang.

Korenman, J. and Wyatt, N. (1996). Group Dynamics in an E-Mail Forum In Herring, S. (ed.), *Computer-Mediated Communication: Linguistic, Social and Cross-Cultural Perspectives*. Amsterdam: John Benjamins, pp. 225-242.

Landow G.P. (1992). *Hypertext*. The Johns Hopkins University Press, Baltimore, USA.

Launspach, S. (1994). "Just my thoughts... " A look at the use of mitigation in electronic discourse. Paper presented at the 8th Annual International Conference on Pragmatics and Language Learning, University of Illinois, Mar 30-Apr 2, 1994, Urbana, IL..

Laurillard, D. (1993). *Rethinking Higher Education*. London: Routledge.

Lea, M. (1992). *Contexts of Computer-Mediated Communication*. London: Harvester-Wheatsheaf.

Lea, M., O'Shea, T. and Fung, P. (1991). *CMC and CSCW: A Bibliography*. Milton Keynes: Open University, 1991.

Lee, C. (1994). PC t'ongsin i chíongsonyondul ui ono saenghwal e mich'inun yonghyang [The Influence of Computer-Mediated Communication on Teenagers]. Unpublished report submitted to the Seoul YMCA.

Lee, K-m. (1963). Kugo píyogibop ui yoksajok yongu [A Study on the History of the Korean Writing System]. Seoul: Hanguk Yonguwon.

Licklider, J.C.R. and R. Taylor. (1968). The computer as a communication device. *Science and Technology*, 76, pp. 21-31.

Linell, P. and T. Luckman. (1991). Asymmetries in dialogue: some conceptual preliminaries, in Marková, I. and K. Foppa (eds.) *Asymmetries of Dialogue*, 1-20. Hemel Hempstead: Harvester Wheatsheaf.

Lyytinen, K., Maaranen, P. and Knuuttila, J. (1994). Groups are not always the same: an analysis of group behaviours in electronic meeting systems. *CSCW* 2:4, pp. 261-284.

Mason, L. (1994). Cognitive and metacognitive aspects in conceptual change by analogy. *Instructional Science*, 22, pp. 157-187.

Mauranen, A. (1993). *Cultural differences in academic writing*. Frankfurt/ Main et al.: Peter Lang.

McCormick, N. B. and J. W. McCormick. (1992). Computer friends and foes: content of undergraduates' electronic mail. *Computers in Human Behavior*, 8, pp. 379-405.

McDonald S. and R. J. Stevenson. (1996). Disorientation in hypertext: the effects of three text structures on navigation performance. *Applied Ergonomics*. 27:1, pp. 61-68.

McDonald S. and R.J. Stevenson. (1997). Hypertext, navigation and cognitive maps: the effects of a map and a contents list on navigation performance as a function of prior knowledge. In D. Harris (ed.) *Engineering Psychology and Cognitive Ergonomics: Interaction of theory and application*. London: Avebury Technical.

Meyrowitz, J. (1997). Shifting Worlds of Strangers: Medium theory and changes in "them" versus "us". *Sociological Inquiry*, 67:1, pp. 59-71.

Miller, G.A. and P.N. Johnson-Laird. (1976). *Language and Perception*. Cambridge, Cambridge University Press.

Murray, D. E. (1988). The context of oral and written language: a framework for mode and medium switching. *Language in Society*, 17, pp. 351-373.

Myers, G. (1989). The Pragmatics of Politeness in Scientific Articles. *Applied Linguistics*, 10:1, pp. 1-35.

Nygren E., Allard A.and M. Lind. (1995). Effects of patterns of highlighted items on list search. Report no. 55, CMD, Uppsala University. http://delfi.cmd.uu.se/papers/55/

Ong, W. J. (1982). *Orality and Literacy: Technologizing of the Word*. London: Routledge.

Park, H-g. (1997). PC tíonsin kesimul ui yusa onojok píyohyon e kwanhan yongu [Research on Paralinguistic Expressions in Newsgroup Postings]. Unpublished M.A. Thesis, Yonsei University.

Pask, G. (1972). A fresh look at cognition and the individual. *International Journal of Man-Machine Studies*, 4, pp. 211-216.

Pask, G. (1975). *Conversation Cognition and Learning*. Amsterdame: Elsevier.

Pask, G. and Scott, B. (1973). CASTE: a system for exhibiting learning strategies and regulating uncertainty. *International Journal of Man-Machine Studies*, 5, pp. 17-52.

Pask, G. and Scott, B. (1972). Learning strategies and individual competence. *International Journal of Man-Machine Studies*, 4, pp. 217-253.

Pask, G. (1976). *Conversation Theory: Applications in Education and Epistemology*. Amsterdam: Elsevier.

Pask, G. (1990). Correspondence, consensus, coherence and the rape of democracy. *Journal of J. Communication and Cognition*, 2-3: 23, pp. 217-228.

Pask, G., Kallikourdis, D. and B. Scott. (1975). The representation of knowables. *International Journal of Man-Machine Studies*, 7, pp. 15-134.

Pask, G. (1968). Man as a system that needs to learn. In Stewart, D. (ed), *Automaton Theory and Learning Systems*, 137-208. London: Academic Press.

Pask, G., Scott, B. and D. Kallikourdis. (1973). A theory of conversations and individuals (exemplified by the learning process on CASTE), *International Journal of Man-Machine Studies*, 5, pp. 443-566.

Pérez-González, L. (1998). The conversational dynamics of interactional dispute in conflictive calls for emergency assistance: a single-case study, in

Sanchez-Macarro, A. and R. Carter (eds.) *Linguistic Choice across Genres: Variation in Spoken and Written English*. Amsterdam: John Benjamins.

Pérez-González, L. (1999) *Towards a dynamic model of discourse: issues of a forensic-oriented study of spoken interaction*. Valencia: Servei de Publicacions de la Universitat de Valencia.

Reichenbach H. (1947). Token-reflexive words. In *Elements of Symbolic Logic*. New York: The Free Press

Reid, E. (1995). Virtual Worlds: Culture and Imagination. In S. G. Jones (ed) *Cybersociety: Computer-mediated communication and community*, pp. 164-183. London: Sage.

Rescher, N. (1973). *Conceptual Idealism*. Oxford: Basil Blackwell.

Rescher, N. (1977). *Methodological Pragmatism*. Oxford: Basil Blackwell.

Rheingold, H. (1992). A Slice of Life in my Virtual Community
http://condorito.metro.msus.edu/sliceoflife.html (accessed 1 May 1997)

Rowntree, D. (1990). *Teaching Through Self-Instruction*. London: Kogan Page.

Rubinstein, J. (1973). *City Police*. New York: Farrar, Straus and Giroux.

Sacks, H. (1992). *Harvey Sacks' Lectures on Conversation 1964-1972*, edited by G. Jefferson. Oxford: Blackwell.

Sacks, H., Schegloff, E. and G. Jefferson. (1974). A simpliest systematics for the organization of Turn-Taking in conversation. *Language*, 50, pp. 697-735.

Sampson, G. (1985). *Writings Systems*. Stanford: Stanford University Press.

Schutz, A. (1962). *Collected Papers*. Vol. 1. Den Hague: Martinus Nijhoff.

Scott, B. (1999). CASTE revisited: principles of course design in a hypertext environment. In Hammond, N. (ed.), *International Handbook of Learning Technology in Psychology*. London: Psychology Press.

Scott, B. (1993). Working with Gordon: developing and applying Conversation Theory (1968-1978). *Systems Research*, 10:3, pp. 167-182.

Searle, J. R. (1976). A Taxonomy of Illucutionary Acts. In J. R. Searle, *Expression and Meaning: Studies in the Theory of Speech Acts*, pp. 1-29. Cambridge: Cambridge University Press.

Sellars W. (1956). Empiricism and the Philosophy of Mind. In Herbert Feigl and Michael Scriven, eds., *Minnesota Studies in the Philosophy of Science, Volume I: The Foundations of Science and the Concepts of Psychology and Psychoanalysis*, pp. 253-329. University of Minnesota Press.
http://csmaclab-www.uchicago.edu/philosophyProject/sellars/epm.html

Shearing, C. (1974). Dial-a-cop: a study of police mobilisation. In Akers, R. and E. Sagarin (eds.) *Crime Prevention and Social Control*, pp. 77-88. London and New York: Praeguer Publishers.

Siegal, J., Dubrovsky, V., Kiesler, S. and T. McGuire. (1986). Group processes in CMC. *Organizational Behaviour and Human Decision Processes*, 37, pp. 157-187.

Smolensky, M. W., Carmody, M. A., and C. G. Halcomb. (1990). The influence of task type, group structure and extraversion on uninhibited speech in CMC. *Computers in Human Behaviour*, 6, pp. 261-272.

Spearman, C. (1923). *The Nature of 'Intelligence' and the Principles of Cognition*. London: Macmillan.

Spears, R., Lea, M. and S. Lee. (1990). De-individuation and group polarisation in CMC. *British Journal of Social Psychology*, 29, pp. 121-134.

Sperber, D. and D. Wilson. (1991). Loose Talk. In S. Davis (ed.), *Pragmatics, a Reader*, 550-563, New York: Oxford University Press.

Sperber, D. and D. Wilson. (1986). *Relevance: Communication and Cognition*. Oxford: Blackwell.

Sproull, L. and S. Kiesler. (1991). *Connections: New Ways of Working in the Networked Organization*. London: MIT Press.

Steele, G. L. (1983). *The Hacker's Dictionary*. New York: Harper and Row.

Stone, A. R. (1991). Will the real body please stand up? Boundary stories about virtual cultures. In M. Benedickt (ed.), *Cyberspace*, pp. 81-118. Cambridge: MIT Press.

Strawson, P. F. (1992). *Analysis and Metaphysics*. London: Oxford University Press.

Swales, J. (1990). *Genre Analysis*. Cambridge: C.U.P.

Tajfel, H. (1981). *Human Groups and Social Categories*. Cambridge: Cambridge University Press.

Trenchs, M. (1990). Writing Strategies in a 2nd-Language - 3 Case Studies of Learners using Electronic Mail. *Canadian Modern Language Review - Revue Canadienne des Langues Vivantes*, 52:3, pp. 464-497.

Turkle, Sherry. (1996) *Life on the Screen: Identity in the Age of the Internet*. London: Weidenfeld and Nicolson.

Turner, J. C., Hogg, M. A., Oakes, P. J., Reicher, S. D. and M.S. (1987). *Rediscovering the Social Group: A Self-Categorisation Theory*. Oxford: Blackwell.

Twine, N. (1991). *Language and the Modern State: The Reform of Written Japanese*. London: Routledge.

Unger, J. M. and J. DeFrancis. (1995). Logographic and Semasiographic Writing Systems: A Critique of Sampson's Classification. In I. Taylor and D. R. Olson (eds.), *Scripts and Literacy: Reading and Learning to Read Alphabets, Syllabaries and Characters*, pp. 45-58. Dordrecht: Kluwer Academic Publishers.

Ventola, E. (1989). Problems of modelling and applied issues within the framework of genre. *Word*, 40:1/2, pp. 129-161.

Ventola, E. (1987). *The Structure of Social Interaction: A Systemic Approach to the Semiotics of Service Encounters*. London: Frances Pinter Publishers.

Vitale, J. (1996). *Cyber Writing*. New York: Amacom.

Wetzstein et al. (1995). *Datenreisende*. Opladen: Westdeutscher Verlag.

Whalen J., D. H. Zimmerman and M. Whalen. (1988). When words fail: a single case analysis. *Social Problems*, 35: 4, 335-362.

Whalen, J. (1994). A technology of order production: computer-aided dispatch in public safety communication. In Ten Have, P. and G. Psathas (eds.) *Situated Order: Studies in the Social Organization of Talk and Embodied Activities*. Washington, D. C.: University Press of America.

Whalen, M. and D. H. Zimmerman. (1987). Sequential and institutional contexts in calls for help. *Social Psychology Quarterly*, 50:2, pp. 172-185.

Whalley, P. (1993). An Alternative Rhetoric for Hypertext. In C. McKnight, A. Dillon, and J. Richardson (eds), *Hypertext: A Psychological Perspective*. Chichester: Ellis Horwood.

Wignall, D. L. (1993). *Computer-Mediated Human Communication: The Identification of Verbal Orality in Written Discourse*. Unpublished Ph.D. Dissertation, The University of Denver.

Wright, P. (1993). To Jump or Not to Jump: Strategy Selection While Reading Electronic Texts. In C. McKnight, A. Dillon, and J. Richardson (eds), *Hypertext: A Psychological Perspective*. Chichester: Ellis Horwood.

Yates, S. and D. Graddol. (1996). "I read this chat is heavy": the discursive construction of identity in CMC. Centre for Language and Communication, Open University: Ms, 1996.

Yates, S. (1996). Oral and Written Linguistic Aspects of Computer Conferencing: A Corpus Based Study. In S. C. Herring (ed), *Computer Mediated Communication*, pp. 29-46. Amsterdam: John Benjamins.

Zimmerman, D. H. and D. Boden. (1991). Structure-in-action: an introduction. In Boden, D. and D. Zimmerman (eds.), *Talk and Social Structure*, pp. 3-21. Oxford: Polity Press.

Zimmerman, D. H. (1984). Talk and its occasion: the case of calling the police. In Schiffrin, D. (ed.) Meaning, Form and Use in Context, pp. 210-228. Washington D. C: Georgetown University Press.

Zimmerman, D. H. (1992a). Achieving context: openings in emergency calls. In Watson, G. and R. Seiler (eds.) *Text in Context*, pp. 35-52. London: Sage Publications.

Zimmerman, D. H. (1992b). The interactional organisation of calls for emergency assistance. In Drew, P. and J. Heritage (eds.) *Talk at Work*, pp. 418-470. Cambridge: Cambridge University Press.